A
PRACTICAL GUIDE
TO COPYRIGHTS
AND TRADEMARKS

A PRACTICAL GUIDE TO COPYRIGHTS AND TRADEMARKS

Frank H. Andorka

OF BAKER & HOSTETLER

Pharos Books are available at special discounts on bulk purchases for sales promotions, premiums, fundraising or educational use. For details, contact the Special Sales Department, Pharos Books, 200 Park Avenue, New York, NY 10166.

Cover design: Elyse Strongin and Eve Sandler
Text design: H. L. Granger

First published in 1989

Library of Congress Cataloging-in-Publication Data
Andorka, Frank H.
    A practical guide to copyrights and trademarks /
Frank H. Andorka.
        p.   cm.
    Includes index.
    ISBN 0-88687-572-2 : $19.95
    1. Copyright—United States. 2. Trademarks—
United States.
    I. Title.
    KF2980.A53   1989
    346.7304'82—dc20   89-8656
    [347.306482]   CIP

World Almanac
An Imprint of Pharos Books
200 Park Avenue
New York, NY 10166

10   9   8   7   6   5   4   3   2   1

ACKNOWLEDGMENTS

Thanks to my associates, Belinda Scrimenti, Scott Keller, Ray Rundelli, and my secretary Joyce Tanski for reviewing the manuscript.

To Jean, Frank, and Claire

CONTENTS

PREFACE

This book is intended as a practical guide to the law of copyright and trademark for media people—those who work for newspapers and magazines, radio and television stations, and publishers. It concentrates on two general areas. First, since members of the media are constantly creating new works, titles, advertising slogans, and the like that are protectible through the laws of copyright and trademark, this book provides guidance on how these newly created and valuable "intellectual properties" can be protected. Second, because members of the media frequently find themselves making use of the works, advertising slogans, and ideas of others, this book provides guidelines as to when such use can be made without authorization from the rights owner, when such use requires permission, and the possible consequences of failing to obtain required permission.

Subjective judgments are frequently required when analyzing the issues raised by a specific set of facts in the copyright/trademark area. Accordingly, while the information in this book should alert the reader to situations where copyright and trademark issues are present, frequently no concrete resolution of an issue will be possible without referring the matter to an attorney who specializes in dealing with intellectual property. And even intellectual property counsel may sometimes find it necessary to answer questions in probabilities rather than certainties.

In 1988 Congress enacted significant revisions of the U.S. copyright and trademark laws. This book reflects the new statutory provisions implemented by these revisions.

CHAPTER ONE

INTRODUCTION

Basic Terms

A *copyright* is a kind of intangible property that protects a work of authorship fixed in any tangible medium of expression. Copyright protection was well established in the law of Great Britain by the time of the American Revolution, and one of the powers vested in the federal government by the U.S. Constitution is the power to "promote the progress of science and useful arts, by securing for a limited time to authors and inventors the exclusive right to their respective writings and discoveries." Copyright protection extends to a broad range of works:

- Literary works (books, newspapers, magazines, short stories, periodical articles; computer software falls in the category of literary works for copyright protection purposes)
- Musical works (including lyrics)
- Dramatic works (including accompanying music)
- Pantomimes and choreographic works

- Pictorial, graphic, and sculptural works (photographs, comic strips and panels, editorial cartoons, paintings, three-dimensional plush toys); See also discussion on page 11 on ownership of copies of an artistic creation
- Motion pictures and other audiovisual works
- Sound recordings

A *trademark* is a word or symbol used in connection with the sale of goods. A *service mark* is a word or symbol used in connection with the advertising or promotion of services. Both types of mark are protected by the same body of law, and a single mark, depending on the way it is used, may function both as a trademark and as a service mark. For example, EXXON might be used as a trademark for motor oil and as a service mark for automotive maintenance services.

A *patent* is a governmental grant to an inventor, for a fixed period of time, of the exclusive right to exploit an invention created by its originator. Patents are frequently confused with copyrights, trademarks, and other types of intellectual property rights, but they are quite separate and distinct forms of property. Only a minimal degree of creativity can produce a work eligible for copyright protection, but a prerequisite to patent protection is "invention"; to be issued a patent, the applicant must have created something new and different from all things created before. The assistance of a specialist patent attorney is required to obtain the issuance of a patent, which is valid for seventeen years from the date of issuance. Patent issues arise only infrequently for members of the media, so patents will not be discussed further in this book.

A *trade name* (also frequently referred to as a *fictitious name*) is a name used by a business to identify itself that is different from the legal name of the individual or entity operating the business. For example, a corporation called Dow Jones & Company Inc., does business under the trade name The Wall Street Journal.

A *corporate name* is the name of an artificial legal entity whose existence is governed by the laws of one of the fifty states.

Relevant Statutes

The current copyright law of the United States is the U.S. Copyright Act of 1976, which took effect January 1, 1978, superseding the U.S. Copyright Act of 1909. Between 1909 and passage of the 1976 act, numerous technological advances occurred which the architects of the 1909 act could not have anticipated. The new act was designed to take into account the vast changes which took place in the first half of the twentieth century in areas such as motion pictures, radio and television broadcasting, and computer technology.

The 1909 act will nevertheless continue to have significance for some time, because it continues to govern all works published prior to January 1, 1978. Under the 1909 act, two kinds of protection were available. Published works were eligible only for federal copyright protection. An unpublished work could be registered with the U.S. Copyright Office and thus gain federal copyright protection, but unregistered unpublished works had common-law copyright protection under the laws of the states, and were not subject to federal protection. The 1976 act specifically provides for federal control in the copyright area; any work created after January 1, 1978—whether published or unpublished, registered or unregistered—is governed by the act. A legal action involving a copyright must be filed in a federal court; state protection for copyrighted works is no longer available.

On October 31, 1988, President Ronald Reagan signed into law a significant amendment to the 1976 act: the Berne Convention Implementation Act of 1988. This act modified the 1976 law in a number of ways deemed necessary by Congress to permit U.S. adherence to the Berne Copyright Convention, an international convention dealing with the protection of copyrights.

The Berne Convention, one of two major international conventions on the protection of copyright, was signed in 1886. Until 1989, the U.S. was the only major commercial country not a signatory to the Berne Convention. In modifying the U.S. domestic copyright law to permit U.S. adherence to Berne, Congress believed that U.S. copyright owners would gain significantly in their ability to protect their copyrights in foreign countries.

The Berne Act took effect on March 1, 1989, the effective date of U.S. adherence to the Berne Convention. Because the implementation act specifically states that it is not retroactive, it will be applicable only to works first published on or after March 1, 1989.

The federal trademark statute, the Lanham Act of 1946, provides for a system of federal registration and protection of trademarks and service marks. Unlike copyright, there is no federal preemption in the trademark/service mark area, and each of the fifty states has a state trademark statute and registry, usually administered by its secretary of state. While a legal action for a federally registered trademark or service mark must be filed in a federal court, legal actions for state-registered marks or unregistered marks may be brought in state courts.

On November 16, 1988, President Reagan signed into law the Trademark Law Revision Act of 1988, the first major overhaul of the Lanham Act since 1946. Changes accomplished by this act became effective November 16, 1989.

International Protection

Protection for U. S. intellectual property rights is available in many foreign countries.

Copyrights. Most major commercial countries (with the notable exceptions of Taiwan and the People's Republic of China) are members of one of two major international copyright conventions, the Berne Convention or the Universal Copyright Convention (UCC), and many countries are members of both. The United States has been a member of the UCC since 1955. As a result of passage of the 1988 Berne Implementation Act the United States became a member the of Berne Convention on March 1, 1989.

If certain requirements are met, under both conventions a copyrighted work owned by a national of one signatory country is entitled to protection in a second signatory country under the laws of the second country. For example, because the United States and France are both signatories to the UCC, a U.S. copyright proprietor who has complied with the requirements of the UCC is entitled to enforce his or her copyright in France under the provisions of the French copyright law. In the great majority of foreign countries adhering to either of the two conventions, it is not necessary for a U.S. copyright owner to take any positive steps (for example, local registration of copyright) to be in a position to enforce copyright.

Trademarks/Service Marks. In sharp contrast to copyright, trademark/service mark rights are almost strictly geographic in scope. Ownership of a trademark or federal registration for a mark in the United States does not give the trademark owner any rights in that mark in, for example, Argentina. If protection in a foreign country is desired, it is almost always necessary to register the mark in that country (the exception is a limited number of marks which can be considered world famous). The Paris Convention, an international treaty dealing with trademark protection, makes it advantageous to file a trademark application in a foreign country within six months of U.S. application because a filing within the required six-month period is awarded a filing date retroactive to the U.S. filing date. The treaty does not, however, eliminate the need for filing.

Copyright and Trademark Law and the Media

Members of the media are among the chief beneficiaries of the copyright and trademark laws. Almost everything that appears in a daily newspaper is eligible for copyright protection: editorials, feature articles, news articles, syndicated columns, comic strips, crossword puzzles, photographs, and even advertisements. Television programs are protected by copyright, whether broadcast nationally by one of the three major commercial networks, syndicated, or produced locally. Copyright is also the major form of protection available to the product of the book publishing industry.

Media-owned trademarks and service marks identify media-created materials in the minds of the public and thus sell media product. A catchy slogan or a distinctive name or logo may encourage consumers to select one media product over another.

Competitive pressures may result in the use of copyrighted materials or trademarks and service marks owned by another. When such an infringement arises it is extremely important that appropriate protection be in place so that copyright or trademark/service mark rights have not somehow been forfeited and can be expeditiously enforced.

While members of the media create their own protected works, they must frequently consider whether they can use copyrighted materials or the trademarks of others without fear of being charged with copyright or trademark infringement. Judgment calls are frequently necessary as to whether a proposed use of someone else's intellectual property is permitted by the law or might result in liability for infringement. An error in judgment can produce extremely unpleasant consequences— including an unnecessary expenditure of thousands of dollars in legal fees, along with the awarding to the injured intellectual property owner of injunctive relief, monetary damages, and other remedies.

CHAPTER 2

PROTECTION OF MEDIA-
CREATED COPYRIGHTS

Creation of Copyrighted Materials

Copyright protection exists when any original work of authorship is "fixed in any tangible medium of expression." When a newspaper article or column is typed on a sheet of paper or into a word processor; when a television news program is videotaped; when a singer's performance is recorded on a phonograph record, a tape, or a compact disc; when a photograph is fixed on a roll of film—in each case copyright protection automatically exists. The author of the work is protected against unauthorized copying from the moment of fixation.

Scope of Copyright Protection

Copyright protection extends only to the expression of an idea, not to the idea itself. Copyright owners are entitled to protection against copying of their copyrighted work; they are

---

For his newspaper Rob writes a brilliant series of investigative columns, which he is sure will win him the Pulitzer Prize. Rob firmly believes the columns have enormous potential for publication in book form and that the movie rights should bring him a minimum advance of a million dollars. To be certain he is on solid ground, Rob asks himself these questions:

1. How can I make sure the columns are protected against being copied without permission by unscrupulous competitors?
2. Is there a way I can prevent someone from relating the facts I uncovered that form the basis for the columns?
3. Do I own the columns, or does my employer own the rights to them?

---

not entitled to prevent someone from borrowing an idea presented in their copyrighted work and then expressing it in the borrower's own fashion. For example, a copyrighted computer program will be expressed so as to cause a computer to act in a certain way. Under the law, the copyright owner of the program is protected against unauthorized copying of that program. However, his or her copyright on the program does not prevent a competitor from independently creating a program that accomplishes the same task, as long as he or she has not copied the original program. The 1976 copyright law specifically states that copyright protection does not extend to any "idea, procedure, process, system, method of operation, concept, principle, or discovery."

To qualify for copyright protection, a work must be "original." The courts have interpreted that word in this context to mean independently created; there is no requirement that a work be novel to be eligible for copyright protection. Not a great deal is required to meet the originality test, but the courts have refused to extend copyright protection to certain types of works on the ground that they are not sufficiently original—single words and short phrases such as names, titles of books or other works, and slogans; symbols or designs; types of lettering; and listings of contents or ingredients. Many materials not subject to copyright protection because of their lack of originality are nevertheless entitled to protection as trademarks or service marks.

Ownership of Copyrighted Materials

Works Created by a Single Author. Ownership of the copyright in a work vests initially in the "author" of the work. The most straightforward situation occurs when a single individual creates a work. For instance, if a single author writes a manuscript, he or she owns the copyright in the manuscript. Similarly, a photographer who snaps a photograph owns copyright in the photograph.

Joint Works. In the case of a *joint work* ("a work prepared by two or more authors with the intention that their contributions be merged into inseparable or interdependent parts of a unitary whole"), the authors are co-owners of the copyright. If a cartoonist and a writer collaborate in producing an installment of a syndicated comic strip, each possesses an undivided half-interest in the copyright in the installment.

Work for Hire. When one person creates a work for or under the instructions of another, copyright ownership may not vest in the creator of the work. If an employee creates a work within the scope of his or her employment, copyright in the work vests in the employer. If an editorial cartoonist, employed by a corporation that publishes a newspaper, within the scope of his or her employment draws an editorial cartoon for publication in the newspaper, the copyright on the editorial cartoon belongs to the employer. In the case of a work created within the scope of the employee-employer relationship just described, the copyrighted work is described as a *work made for hire*.

The work-made-for-hire concept is also important in a second category of cases where creation of a work is commissioned by a person other than the author and the author is not an employee of the commissioning party. In such circumstances, the commissioning party is considered the author and therefore the owner of copyright in the commissioned work, unless the parties expressly agree in writing that copyright in the work will vest in the author. This seems simple enough, but the issue of ownership is complicated by a restriction in the copyright law of the definition of works made for hire falling within this second category to works "specially ordered or commissioned for use as a contribution to a collective work, as a part of a motion picture or other audiovisual work, as a translation, as a supplementary work, as a compilation, as an instructional text, as a test, as answer material for a test, or as an atlas." The clear implication is that if a work does not fall within one of the enumerated types, it cannot be a second-category work made for hire, and copyright in such a work does not automatically vest in the commissioning person. The United States Supreme court, in a 1989 decision, confirmed that the statute means what it says—a work created by an independent contractor cannot be a work for hire unless it one of the types of works listed in the statute.

The issue created by this definition can be important. If a television station commissions a video photographer to videotape a local high school football game, it might be assumed by the parties that, as the commissioning party, the station is the owner of the copyright on the resulting videotape. However, since the videotape does not fall within any of the categories of works made for hire defined by the copyright law, the videotape copyright would actually vest in the photographer. When the person commissioning creation of a work that does not fall within one of the possible types of "works made for hire" contained in the legal definition wishes to own the copyright on the work, he or she can obtain title only by having the author of the work execute a written assignment of copyright in his or her favor. Such a written assignment should be obtained, as a matter of caution, when there is any doubt which party is to own the copyright on a commissioned work or whether the type of work commissioned falls within the statutory definition of a work made for hire.

Assignments of Copyright. A copyright is property and, like other kinds of property, can be transferred by written assignment, under a will, or by the laws of intestate succession. Any assignment of copyright should be in writing and should clearly identify the work or works covered by the assignment and indicate that the copyrights are being transferred. Prior to the 1988 amendment of the copyright law by the Berne Convention Implementation Act, copyright assignments had to be recorded with the U.S. Copyright Office in Washington, D.C., so that the assignee of the copyright appeared as record owner; this recording was a prerequisite to enforcement of the copyright. Now recording of transfers is voluntary.

Ownership of Copy

The proprietor of copyright in a work has no right to prevent transfer of an authorized copy of the work by its owner. For example, while a sculptor may retain copyright ownership in his sculpture and can prevent it from being copied, he cannot prevent the owner of the sculpture from transferring to another person title to the actual sculpture. This concept, sometimes referred to as the *first-sale doctrine*, means that once a copyright owner has transferred possession of a copy, he has no further right to control its use, and the owner of the copy can make whatever use of the copy he desires, as long as no copying occurs. The rationale is that the copyright owner is entitled to benefit from the initial sale of his copyrighted work, but not from subsequent sales by the first purchaser.

A traditional analysis of one of the possible consequences of the first-sale doctrine would run as follows. Assume an individual purchases a copyrighted greeting card. The purchaser may do whatever he or she wants with the artwork on the card. The purchaser may frame the artwork on the card and sell it as a framed print. The purchaser may cut out portions of the card and place them on pendants or keychains, which he or she may then sell. The purchaser may not, however, make copies of the copyrighted artwork from the card by, for example, making additional cards or picturing in catalogs the pendants or keychains produced from the copyrighted card.

Some doubt has been shed on the foregoing traditional analysis by a 1988 decision of the United States Court of Appeals for the Ninth Circuit (an intermediate federal appellate court with jurisdiction over a number of western states, including California). That case held that a defendant who cut copyrighted artwork out of a book, glued it to ceramic tiles, and sold the ceramic tiles infringed the copyright owner's exclusive right to create derivative works based on the artwork. A traditional first-sale analysis would have excused the defendant from liability for infringement. If federal courts choose to follow this Ninth Circuit decision, the scope of the first-sale doctrine will be severely limited.

Notice of Copyright After Effective Date of the Berne Act

Use of Notice Voluntary. As of the effective date of the Berne Act, March 1, 1989, use of a copyright notice (a notice identifying the year of first publication of the work and the copyright owner) is voluntary; copyright protection can no longer be forfeited through publication without notice. This major change in U.S. law implemented by the Berne Act occurred because a domestic copyright notice requirement was inconsistent with the prerequisites to U.S. adherence to the Berne Convention.

Continued Advisability of Use of Notice. Despite the Berne Act's elimination of possible forfeiture of copyright protection through failure to use a copyright notice, it remains advisable to use a notice. The appearance of notice on a work may deter potential infringers from making infringing copies. A notice may be useful in identifying authorized copies, and in an infringement action use of a notice may nullify a defendant's claim of innocent infringement. Finally, use of the UCC form of notice may preserve protection in a small number of foreign countries that are signatories to the UCC but not to the Berne Convention. An appropriate notice would appear as follows: © 1989 [copyright owner's name].

Notice of Copyright Prior to the Berne Act

Ed, an editor for a New York publishing house, in the fall of 1988 was reviewing the final galleys of a blockbuster novel for which his employer had paid a $1.5-million advance. Ed observed a copyright notice that he believed gave the copyright page a cluttered look. He deleted it and returned the galleys to the printer, and 250,000 hardcover copies of the book were printed, for distribution in January 1989, without copyright notices. Why was Ed's employer extremely displeased?

While the Berne Act made the use of a copyright notice optional, under earlier law failure to use a copyright notice could result in forfeiture of copyright protection. For that reason, a fairly detailed discussion of the copyright notice requirements of prior law will be useful here.

Notice Requirement. Former law required that a specified notice of copyright be placed on a work protected by the copyright law whenever it was "published in the United States or elsewhere by authority of the copyright owner." The U.S. requirement of the use of a copyright notice as a prerequisite to continued protection was unusual. No other important commercial country imposed copyright-notice requirements, and foreign nationals often were unable to understand the emphasis U.S. copyright owners placed on publication with appropriate notice.

Form of Notice. The form of notice specified by the law as it stood prior to the effective date of the Berne Act contained three elements:

- The word *Copyright*, the abbreviation *Copr.*, or the copyright symbol ©
- The year of first publication of the work
- The name of the copyright proprietor, "or an abbreviation by which the name can be recognized, or a generally known alternative designation of the owner."

The law required that sound recordings (phonograph records or tape cassettes, for example) bear a notice containing the same elements, except that the symbol   had to be used in place of the symbol © or the abbreviation *Copr.* or the word *Copyright*. One of the requirements of the UCC for obtaining automatic protection in member countries is the use of a notice meeting the former notice requirements of the act, utilizing the copyright symbol © rather than the word *Copyright* or the abbreviation *Copr.*

Placement of Notice. The 1909 act, and regulations issued by the Copyright Office under it, contained stringent requirements as to the placement of copyright notice. In contrast, the law prior to the Berne Act required only that notice be "affixed to the copies in such manner and location as to give reasonable notice of the claim of copyright."

Consequences of Publication Without Notice. Under the 1909 act, publication of a work without a copyright notice resulted in forfeiture of copyright protection. In enacting the Copyright Act of 1976, Congress intentionally sought to lessen these harsh consequences, and that law contained a number of provisions which gave the copyright owner an opportunity to avoid forfeiture of copyright protection in the event of publication without notice. Thus, the absence of a copyright notice on a work published prior to March 1, 1989, does not establish without question that the work is in the public domain because copyright protection has been forfeited.

Publication with Incorrect Notice. Under the law before the Berne Act, publication of a work with a copyright notice containing an incorrect name for the copyright owner or an incorrect year did not invalidate copyright in the work. A work published prior to March 1, 1989, with incorrect information in the copyright notice cannot be assumed to have been placed in the public domain.

Deposit and Registration

Deposit with Library of Congress. In order to provide the Library of Congress with a wide-ranging collection of all works being published in the U.S., two complete copies of the best edition of any work published in the United States must be deposited with the Library of Congress within three months after publication. If a deposit is not made within the required period, the Register of Copyrights (the chief executive of the Copyright Office) is entitled to make a written demand that the copyright owner make the required deposit. If deposit is not made within three months from the date of the demand, the copyright owner may be subject to a fine.

Registration. Registration of copyright in a work, whether the work is published or unpublished, may be made at any time while the copyright remains in effect. Registration is accomplished by filing with the Copyright Office an appropriate Copyright Office form, a ten-dollar application fee, and a deposit consisting (for an unpublished work) of one copy or (for a published work) two complete copies of the best edition of the work. In the case of certain types of works where depositing complete copies would be difficult (for example, motion pictures or sculptures) the Copyright Office by regulation permits the deposit of photographs or other identifying material. (See Appendix A for specific information on obtaining forms, with relevant addresses and phone numbers.)

The deposit of copies accompanying a copyright application satisfies the requirements of the copyright law for depositing copies with the Library of Congress.

In the case of a work which is a contribution to a collective work, the deposit can be one complete copy of the best edition of the entire collective work.

To save authors of large numbers of works published frequently from having to pay large copyright registration fees, the copyright law permits single registration of a group of related works. Thus, for example, daily editions of a newspaper may be gathered and registered with the Copyright Office by completing and filing a single application form and paying a single registration fee. The copyright law also permits single registration by an individual author of various contributions to periodicals within a twelve-month period, also for a single ten-dollar registration fee.

The Copyright Office publishes a number of registration application forms covering different types of works: Form TX for nondramatic literary works (books, magazines, etc.); Form VA for works of the visual arts (photographs, paintings, etc.); Form SR for sound recordings; Form PA for works of the performing arts (musical compositions, motion pictures, etc.); and Form SE for serials (magazines, newsletters, etc.). Copyright application forms can be obtained free of charge from the Information Section LM-455, Copyright Office, The Library of Congress Washington, D.C. 20559. Each different application form is accompanied by detailed instructions explaining how the form should be completed. Legal assistance is usually not needed to register copyright.

Assuming that the copyright application is properly completed and the necessary deposit and fee are received, the Copyright Office will issue a copyright registration certificate within a month or two after the date of filing of the application. This consists of the original application with a seal attached and a registration number assigned. The effective date of the registration is the date the completed application and required accompanying material are received by the Copyright Office. When introduced in a legal proceeding, the copyright registration certificate is prima facie evidence that the named registrant owns the copyright covered by the registration.

> On the evening news Andy delivers a scathing I-Team report, ten minutes in length, on corruption in the city's distribution of government cheese. Andy's station routinely tapes its own news programs and runs a copyright notice across the screen at the end of each program, but the copyrights on the programs are not usually registered. Six months later Chad, Andy's archrival at a competing station, runs Andy's investigative piece in its entirety on his own news program, followed by commentary ridiculing Andy's reporting skills. Andy calls his station's counsel and requests that he immediately file suit against Chad for copyright infringement. Why does Andy's counsel advise him that suit cannot be filed immediately?

Reasons for Registration. The most important reason for registering a copyright is the fact that registration is a prerequisite to instituting legal proceedings for infringement of a U.S.-origin copyrighted work. Registration is further encouraged by a provision in the copyright law that no statutory damages or attorneys' fees may be awarded to the copyright owner for infringement of copyright in an unpublished work if infringement commenced before copyright in the work was registered, or for infringement of a published work which began after first publication and before registration, unless registration was effected within three months after the date of first publication.

Under the Berne Act, registration is no longer a prerequisite to filing an action for infringement of a work of foreign origin.

Duration of Copyright

Current Law. Copyright comes into existence on creation of a work and lasts for a period equal to the life of the author plus fifty years. In the case of a joint work created by two or more persons, the term of copyright extends for a period of fifty years following the death of the last surviving author. Copyright in works for hire and anonymous and pseudonymous works subsists for a period of seventy-five years from the date of first publication of the work, or one hundred years from the date of creation of the work, whichever is shorter.

> Wanda, wanting to produce a children's program to fill an hour's time during her station's broadcast day, creates a screenplay based on a children's book first published in 1920. Wanda reasons that a book initially published that long ago must be in the public domain. Why is she exposing herself and her station to possible legal difficulties?

Renewal Copyright Under the 1909 Act. These provisions on duration of copyright discussed above apply only to works created after January 1, 1978. The 1909 Copyright Act remains relevant, and will remain so for a considerable period of time, in determining the length of copyright protection available for a work created before January 1, 1978. The 1909 act provided for a protection period of twenty-eight years from the date of publication, or twenty-eight years from the date of registration in the case of certain unpublished works. Following this initial twenty-eight-year term, an additional renewal copyright, also for twenty-eight years, was available. Current copyright law retains the concept of initial copyright/renewal copyright for works published prior to January 1, 1978, but extends the renewal term to forty-seven years, to give works first published prior to January 1, 1978, a total period of protection of seventy-five years, roughly equivalent to the extended protection now given to works created after January 1, 1978.

The renewal copyright mechanism in the 1909 act was designed to give authors who transferred ownership of copyright a second chance to reap the benefits of a popular work. If an author transferred only the copyright in his or her work, the transferee obtained only the initial twenty-eight-year term of copyright, and the renewal copyright continued to belong to the author. Thus, if an author in a poor bargaining position transferred to another party for a relatively small sum the copyright in his or her work and the work subsequently became valuable, after expiration of the initial twenty-eight-year copyright term the author would be in a position to obtain the renewal copyright in the work and reap the benefits of continued exploitation of the work after the initial term. The transferee of copyright for the initial twenty-eight-year term of protection would have no interest in the work during the twenty-eight-year renewal term.

The renewal copyright provisions of the 1909 act did not make clear whether an author could assign both the initial twenty-eight-year term of copyright and the twenty-eight-year renewal term simultaneously. If the author were able to make such a simultaneous assignment, the second chance represented by the renewal copyright would have little value, since the author would be likely to bargain it away for little compensation at the same time he or she assigned the initial twenty-eight-year term. Court decisions construing the 1909 act permitted an author making a transfer of the initial term of copyright in a work to transfer the renewal copyright at the same time. This gave the transferee, not the author, the right to exploit the work during the twenty-eight-year renewal term and effectively undermined the purpose of the renewal copyright concept. Also, with regard to certain types of works including composite works (periodicals and encyclopedias, for example) works copyrighted by a corporate body, and works created by an employer for hire, renewal copyright vested in the person obtaining the initial copyright and not in the author.

In the case of all other types of works, and absent a transfer of renewal copyright, renewal copyright vested in the author of the work. To acquire this vested interest in the renewal copyright, the author had to survive until the commencement of the twenty-eight-year renewal copyright term. The recipient of an author's renewal copyright obtained nothing at the time of the transfer except the right to claim ownership of the renewal copyright if the author lived until the commencement date of the twenty-eight-year renewal copyright term.

If the author failed to survive, however, the renewal copyright vested in survivors of the author in order of priority assigned under the copyright law. The first class of persons entitled to succession to renewal copyright was the author's widow or widower and children. If the author left no widow or widower or children but left a will, renewal copyright vested in the executor of the author's estate. If the author left no widow or widower or children and died without a will, renewal copyright passed to the author's next of kin, as determined by the laws of intestacy of the state where the author lived at the time of death. In summary, if an author assigned a renewal copyright but then died before the beginning of the renewal copyright term, the renewal copyright would not belong to the person to whom the author had transferred it but rather to individuals (most likely relatives) designated by the copyright law.

To secure a renewal copyright, a renewal copyright application must be filed with the Copyright Office during the one-year period prior to expiration of the original term of copyright. If a renewal application is not timely and properly filed during this one-year time period, the copyrighted work loses copyright protection and goes into the public domain. Once a work is in the public domain, it may be copied freely, without permission from the author or other owner of the initial twenty-eight-year term of copyright.

Terminations of Transfer. Because the renewal copyright mechanism embodied in the 1909 act had failed to accomplish its intended purpose, in enacting the Copyright Act of 1976 Congress sought an alternative means of permitting an author in an unequal bargaining position to have a second opportunity to benefit from the popularity of his or her work. The alternative selected is found in the termination of transfer provisions of the law, which apply to works created on or after January 1, 1978. These provisions specifically prohibit the transfer or waiving of termination rights prior to the date they vest. Thus, while under prior law an improvident author could assign away at the same time both the initial and renewal terms of copyright, under current law an author is unable to assign away his or her termination of transfer rights, even if he or she wishes to do so.

Current copyright law provides that any transfer or license of copyright executed by an author after January 1, 1978, may be terminated. The right of termination may be exercised (by the author or certain designated individuals; see below) at any time during the five-year period commencing on the date thirty-five years from the date of execution of the transfer or license. Alternatively, if the author has assigned or licensed to the transferee the right to publish the work, the five-year period during which the right of termination may be exercised commences on the date thirty-five years from the date of publication or forty years from the date of execution of the grant, whichever is earlier.

Grants executed before January 1, 1978, may be terminated during the five-year period beginning at the end of fifty-six years from the date copyright was originally secured or beginning January 1, 1978, whichever is later.

If the author of a work is alive at the time a right of termination arises and properly exercises the termination right, the rights originally granted to the author's transferee revert to the author. In the case of a work created by joint authors, a termination of transfer may be exercised only by a majority of the authors.

If the author is not alive at the time the right to terminate a transfer arises, the termination right may be exercised by the author's widow or widower, who owns the entire termination interest if the author is not survived by children or grandchildren. If the author leaves a widow or widower and children or grandchildren, the widow or widower owns one half of the termination right, while the children or grandchildren own the other half. Where the author leaves no widow or widower but leaves surviving children, the children possess equal rights in the termination interest. If an author leaves both children and children of a deceased child, the children of the deceased child (the author's grandchildren) possess the interest of the deceased child.

Exercise of a termination right must be accomplished in accordance with the terms of the Copyright Act of 1976. The termination notice must be in writing, and all persons having an interest in the termination right who are joining in exercising the termination right must sign the notice. The termination notice, which must specify the effective date of termination, must be served on the party owning the grant being terminated. The notice of termination must be recorded with the Copyright Office prior to the effective date of termination.

Enforcement of Copyrights

Paul, putting together a tourist guide to southern California, decides to illustrate it with likenesses of a well-known cartoon mouse. Paul tells himself that because the illustrations are a very small portion of his entire book, the consequences will not be serious if the owner of the mouse's likeness complains. Why is Paul likely to be unpleasantly surprised?

Acts Constituting Infringement. Copyright infringement occurs when someone, without authorization from the copyright owner, exercises any of the rights in a work belonging exclusively to the copyright owner. Unauthorized reproduction; preparation of derivative works; distribution by sale, rental, lease, or lending; public performance; or public display can all constitute acts of infringement. While copying of a work is required for infringement to occur, it is not necessary that the copying occur in the same medium as the original work. For example, a motion picture based on a copyrighted novel and produced without permission of the copyright owner would infringe the copyright on the novel on which the motion picture is based.

Persons Entitled to Enforce Copyrights. An action for infringement of copyright may be brought only in the federal courts by the proprietor of copyright in the work or by a party possessing any one of the exclusive rights belonging to a copyright proprietor. If a copyright owner has granted a manufacturer an exclusive license to reproduce a copyrighted work of art on a T-shirt, the licensee would be entitled to take action against infringers making unauthorized reproductions of the work of art on T-shirts unless prohibited from doing so by his or her contract with the copyright holder.

Remedies for Copyright Infringement. Having proved in an infringement lawsuit that he or she owns the copyright, that the infringer had access to the copyrighted work, and that the entire copyrighted work had been copied or that there was substantial similarity between the copyrighted work and the infringer's work, the copyright proprietor is entitled to the following remedies:

- **Injunctive Relief.** An injunction granted by a federal court in a copyright infringement action is operative throughout the U.S. and is enforceable by contempt proceedings.
- **Seizure of Infringing Copies and Other Materials.**

While a lawsuit for infringement is pending (that is, before the trial court has rendered its final decision in the case) a federal court may order seizure or impounding of all copies of the infringing work and any materials (for example, molds, tapes, or films) from which the infringing copies can be made.

- **Damages and Profits.** The copyright owner is entitled to recover from an infringer both actual damages suffered as a result of the infringing conduct plus any profits earned by the infringer through the acts of infringement, or, alternatively, statutory damages. To establish profits earned by an infringer from his or her infringing activity, the copyright proprietor need only put into evidence proof of the infringer's total revenues from exploitation of the infringing work. It is then left to the infringer to produce evidence of any expenses to be deducted from total revenues in calculating profits.

- **Statutory Damages.** This provision of the act provides copyright owners with an exceptional optional weapon to use against infringers. At any time in the course of an infringement action before a final judgment is entered, the copyright proprietor is entitled to elect to recover from the infringer, instead of the infringer's profits and actual damages, statutory damages in a range, at the court's discretion, from $500 to $20,000 for each infringement ($250 to $10,000 before the effective date of the Berne Act). If the copyright owner proves to the court that the infringer's acts of infringement were willful, the upper limit of the statutory-damages award for each infringement may be set as high as $100,000, again at the court's discretion ($50,000 prior to the effective date of the Berne Act). Conversely, if the infringer can convince the court that he or she had no reason to believe that his or her acts were infringing, the statutory damages may be reduced to $200 per infringement ($100 before the effective date of the Berne Act). Thus, even in an infringement in which the copyright owner is unaware of the scope of the defendant's infringing activity, or where there is difficulty proving the defendant's actual damages and profits, or where the infringer has actually lost money as a result of infringing conduct, the copyright owner can still credibly insist that he or she is entitled to a monetary recovery. The statutory damages provisions greatly assist copyright owners in obtaining monetary compensation from infringers and can be used to encourage negotiated monetary settlements even before litigation is begun.

- **Costs and Attorneys' Fees.** The court may allow one party in an infringement action to recover from the other full costs and may also, at its discretion, allow the prevailing party to recover reasonable attorneys' fees from the other party.

Statute of Limitations

The statute of limitations for a civil copyright infringement action is three years. Suit must be filed within three years of the date an infringement occurred; otherwise the copyright owner's ability to sue against the infringer is lost.

Criminal Infringement of Copyright

Infringement of a copyright "willfully and for purposes of commercial advantage or private financial gain" is a federal crime. Persons guilty of infringement of copyright for most types of works are subject to a fine of not more than $10,000 or imprisonment for up to one year. In the case of criminal infringement of copyrights in sound recordings or motion pictures, the penalties are increased to a maximum $25,000 fine and one year imprisonment for the first offense and a maximum $50,000 fine or two years imprisonment or both for any subsequent infringement. On conviction of a criminal infringer, the court handling the criminal infringement proceeding is entitled to order the destruction of all infringing copies or materials used for producing the infringing copies.

> Patty observes that a poster produced from a photograph of a scenic vista near her hometown is selling extremely well in local shops. Patty decides there is money to be made and that she will print her own edition of the poster. She buys one of the posters and sets about printing several thousand copies. Patty notes the poster bears a copyright notice in the name of a prominent local photographer. She shrugs and says "Big deal—it's not as if it's a crime." Why may Patty have turned herself into a common criminal?

The following activities are also categorized as criminal conduct: fraudulent placement of a copyright notice or fraudulent distribution of materials bearing false copyright notices; fraudulent removal of copyright notices; knowingly making false representations of material facts in connection with applications to register copyrights.

Recording of Copyrights with U.S. Customs

The importation of infringing copies of works protected under copyright law is prohibited, with enforcement entrusted to the U.S. Customs Service. To take advantage of customs protection against importation of infringing copies, the copyright owner must first register his or her copyright with the Copyright Office and then, in accordance with customs regulations, file with the Customs Service a certified copy of the registration certificate along with a specified number of copies of the copyrighted work. On receipt of these materials and a stipulated filing fee, U.S. Customs will distribute a circular to all customs offices, instructing them to bar importation of materials infringing the protected copyright. When such an attempted importation of infringing copies is noted, customs offices around the United States will block their importation and notify the copyright owner that such importation is being attempted. Infringing copies may be seized by customs and thus prevented from reaching the U.S. market or, alternatively, customs may order the infringer to return the infringing copies to the country of origin. If the importer attempts to convince customs that the copies sought to be imported are not infringing, the copyright owner has the right to present arguments in opposition. Customs must then make a formal decision whether or not the importer's copies are infringing. Customs may require the copyright owner to post a bond to protect the importer from any damage suffered as a consequence of delay of importation should it ultimately be determined that the copyright owner was not justified in seeking exclusion of the items.

Customs interference with the importation of infringing copies is spotty, and recording of copyright with U.S. Customs is not a panacea for dealing with an infringement problem. Recording is, however, one useful tool for dealing with such a problem, particularly when the copyright owner is faced with a massive number of infringements, such as may arise with popular toy items.

CHAPTER 3

USE OF COPYRIGHTED MATERIALS OF OTHERS

The decision to publish a photograph in a newspaper or magazine, to broadcast a song as part of a news program, or to quote extensively from a book in connection with a documentary can raise issues of possible copyright infringement.

Determining if a Work is Protected by Copyright

When use of the work of another is contemplated, it is essential to determine whether the work is protected by copyright. If the work bears a copyright notice, it may be easy to determine whether copyright protection still exists for the work, but determination may also prove difficult.

If a work bears a copyright notice earlier than 1912, it is safe to assume that the work is in the public domain and may be freely copied without seeking authorization from anyone. If a work bears an after-1958 copyright notice, it can be assumed that the work is still subject to copyright protection, either because it is in its initial twenty-eight-year term of copyright, under the provisions of the 1909 act, or protected for the terms of copyright specified under the Copyright Act of 1976 if created after January 1, 1978.

Works published between 1912 and 1958 may or may not be in the public domain. The 1909 act provided for an initial twenty-eight-year term of copyright, plus a twenty-eight-year renewal. If a pre-1958 work was published with notice of copyright (the copyright owner thus securing statutory copyright protection), copyright would subsist for a period of twenty-eight years, but the work would then go into the public domain unless the owner applied for and obtained his or her twenty-eight year renewal copyright. Copyright protection for a work first published in 1940 with an appropriate copyright notice would have expired in 1968 unless the owner of the renewal copyright interest at that time filed for and obtained a renewal copyright registration from the Copyright Office.

If examination of a copyrighted work reveals a copyright notice dated earlier than 1958 and no information on renewal copyright, the records of the Copyright Office must be checked to determine whether the copyright on the work has been renewed in order to ascertain whether permission to reproduce the work is necessary.

Determining whether a work is in the public domain is further complicated by the fact that the Copyright Act of 1976 granted owners of copyright in works for which, under the 1909 act, the twenty-eight-year renewal term would have expired between September 19, 1962, and December 31, 1976, an additional nineteen years of renewal copyright protection, making such protection available for a total of forty-seven years. A work first published in 1940, eligible for renewal of copyright in 1968, would qualify for the extended forty-seven-year renewal term provided for in the 1976 act and copyright protection would continue until 2015.

Even if a work does not bear a copyright notice, it cannot be assumed that the work is in the public domain. As discussed earlier, if a work was first published prior to March 1, 1989, without a copyright notice, there were a number of saving provisions in the 1976 act that may have enabled the copyright owner to prevent the work from becoming public domain. Works published after March 1, 1989, are not required to bear a notice, so lack of notice does not provide a dependable clue as to whether the work is protected by copyright. If a work lacking copyright notice is copied innocently, the copier may avoid liability for infringement, but under the current act the copier bears the burden of proving that he or she was misled by the absence of a notice into believing that the work was not protected by copyright.

Permission from the copyright owner, preferably in writing, is required in most instances for the reproduction of a copyrighted work. While identifying the copyright owner may be a fairly easy task in the case of a recently published work, it may prove extremely difficult for an older work, primarily because of the provisions of the 1909 act and the 1976 act relating to ownership of renewal copyrights. If the author or other original holder of the initial twenty-eight-year term of copyright has died, it may be virtually impossible to identify and locate all of the persons who were entitled under the statutes to inherit the renewal copyright interest.

When Copying a Copyrighted Work Without Permission Is Excused

Under certain limited circumstances, copying of a copyrighted work is permitted without authorization from the copyright owner.

Fair Use. Fair use of a copyrighted work is copying that is excused for reasons of public policy. If a particular act of copy-

> Ernie is extremely taken by an editorial cartoon published in a rival newspaper and reprints the entire cartoon on his own editorial page. When his editorial assistant, seeing a copyright notice on the cartoon, suggests that reprinting it without permission might not be a good idea, Ernie responds, "It's news, it's a fair use, so they can't complain." Why does Ernie subsequently regret his statement?

ing is a "fair use," the copier is not liable to the copyright owner for infringement. Created by the courts under the 1909 act, the fair use defense is part of the current copyright statute. Fair use is of sufficient importance to those in the media to justify quoting the fair use provision of the act (17 U.S.C.§107) in its entirety:

> Notwithstanding the provisions of section 106 [defining the exclusive rights the act grants the copyright owner], the fair use of a copyrighted work, including such use by reproduction in copies or phonorecords or by any other means specified by that section, for purposes such as criticism, comment, news reporting, teaching (including multiple copies for classroom use), scholarship, or research, is not an infringement of copyright. In determining whether the use made of a work in any particular case is a fair use the factors to be considered shall include—
>
> (1) the purpose and character of the use, including whether such use is of a commercial nature or is for non-profit educational purposes;
> (2) the nature of the copyrighted work;
> (3) the amount and substantiality of the portion used in relation to the copyrighted work as a whole; and
> (4) the effect of the use upon the potential market for or value of the copyrighted work.

The copyright law does not enumerate all the types of uses that may be fair use. Nor are the listed factors to be taken into consideration in determining whether a use is a fair use all-inclusive. Whether or not a particular use is a fair use depends very much on the facts peculiar to each case. It is frequently difficult to predict whether a fair use defense will succeed in a particular case.

Examples of uses that would almost always be considered fair uses include:

- the quoting of small portions of a copyrighted book in connection with a review of the book
- quoting a portion of a copyrighted speech in an article published in a scholarly journal
- displaying a copyrighted painting in connection with a television news report on the artist

A number of courts have stated that it is not possible for a use to be fair if the copyright owner's entire work is appropriated. Thus copying a complete copyrighted poem or cartoon or photograph, particularly for commercial purposes, will likely not be considered a fair use.

Parody and satire frequently figure in discussions of the fair use defense. A court may find that a parody of a copyrighted work does not infringe the copyright because the parody is a fair use. In making this determination, the court may well focus on the four factors listed in the statute as requiring analysis when a fair use defense is raised. A parody is a writing in which the language and style of an author is imitated, particularly for comic effect. It is not a parody to adopt or use a copyrighted work for the purpose of communicating the copier's own views. Writing new lyrics for a copyrighted musical work to permit the copier to express his or her own political commentary does not justify copying the musical work. Incorporating a popular copyrighted cartoon character in an editorial cartoon to express criticism or approval of governmental policies would not be a parody of that character. In both of the cases just described, a court in an action brought by the owner of the copyright in the copied work would likely hold the copier liable for infringement.

Stu is incensed to find that his college library has photo-copied his copyrighted article from a scholarly historical journal and provided the copy to Stu's rival for the chairmanship of the history department. His rival intends to use the copy in connection with a treatise he is writing on the same subject as the article. Aware that his copyright in the article prevents unauthorized copying, Stu seeks to make trouble for his rival by threatening him with legal action for copyright infringement. His rival seems unconcerned by Stu's threat. Why?

Copying by Libraries and Archives. Under an extremely complex provision in the copyright law, copying of copyrighted materials by libraries and archives without permission from the copyright owner is permitted. The copying must take place "without any purpose of direct or indirect commercial advantage." The library or archive claiming the exemption must be open to the public and any copies made must reproduce the copyright notice appearing on the copied work.

In addition to these general requirements for the exemption to be available to a library or an archive, the following specific requirements and provisions must be followed:

- With regard to unpublished works, copies may be made solely for the purpose of preserving the work or for research use in another library or archive.
- Published works may be duplicated solely for purposes of replacing copies that are damaged, deteriorating, lost, or stolen, if a replacement copy cannot be obtained at a fair price.
- Libraries may copy works when a library user or another library requests a copy of no more than one article from a copyrighted compilation or periodical or a copy of a small portion of any other copyrighted work if the copy becomes the property of the requesting party; the library

making the copy believes the copy will not be used for a purpose other than private study, scholarship, or research; and the library prominently displays, at the place where orders for copies are accepted, a copyright warning prescribed by the Register of Copyrights. Copies for users may also be made of entire works or substantial portions of works, under the same two conditions, provided the library determines that a copy of the work cannot be obtained at a fair price.

- Libraries are not liable for copyright infringement resulting from patrons' use of copying equipment located on library premises if the equipment displays an appropriate copyright warning.

- Simply because a library is exempted from liability for copying as a result of a request for a copy of a copyrighted work by a library user does not mean that the user is necessarily exempt from liability for infringement if the user makes a use of the work exceeding the bounds of fair use.

- The library/archive exemption does not apply to musical works; pictorial, graphic, or sculptural works; or to motion pictures and audiovisual works unless such works are included within other types of works (such as periodical issues) to which the exemption applies.

Exemption for Certain Performances and Displays. Another very complex provision of the copyright law exempts certain performances and displays from liability for copyright infringement. Exempted performances and displays include:

- The performance or display of a work by teachers or pupils as part of face-to-face teaching activities in a classroom of a nonprofit educational institution does not infringe the copyright interest of the owner of the performed or displayed work. Thus, pupils in a drama class may perform portions of a copyrighted play without liability to the play's copyright owner. Wholesale copying of a printed version of the play for use by pupils is, however, not permitted. The legislative history of the provision states that the statute does not "sanction the unauthorized reproduction of copies or phonorecords for the purpose of classroom performance or display."

- Similarly, literary or musical works may be performed or displayed in the course of a transmission as part of systematic instructional activities of a governmental body or nonprofit educational institution, so long as the performance or display relates to the teaching content of the transmission and the transmission is made primarily for reception in classrooms, to disabled persons, or to employees of governmental bodies.

- Performance or display of a copyrighted work of a religious nature in the course of a religious meeting does not result in liability for infringement.

- Performance of a copyrighted work without any commercial purpose and without payment of any fee to the performers is exempt from liability for copyright infringement as long as there is no admission charge to the performance or the net proceeds are used for educational, religious, or charitable purposes.

- The performance of a copyrighted transmission (*transmit* means to communicate a copyrighted work by any device or process whereby images or sounds are received beyond the place from which they are sent) in a public place does not result in liability for infringement as long as it occurs through equipment of a kind commonly used in private homes, no charge is made to see or hear the transmission, and no further transmission is made to the public. A commercial establishment may thus legally transmit on its premises copyrighted music and other copyrighted elements of a radio broadcast (news programs, talk shows, etc.) so long as it uses only the required single receiving apparatus. The same establishment's installation of a more complex sound system could result in liability for infringement.

- Performance of a musical work by a governmental body

or "non-profit agricultural or horticultural organization" in the course of an annual fair produces no liability for infringement.

- Performance of copyrighted music by an establishment engaged in the retail sale of records is not an infringement of copyright.
- Certain performances, outlined in the statute, directed at blind or other handicapped persons are exempt from liability for copyright infringement.

> Paula has collaborated with Clarence to create the hit Broadway musical of the year, entitled *Kansas!* They become extremely upset when a friend advises them that the musical is being performed, without their permission, at the Kansas State Fair in Topeka. Their counsel advises Paula and Clarence that they are not entitled to any compensation for the unauthorized performance of the musical. What could they have done to avoid finding themselves in this position?

To prevent a copyright owner from being forced to make an involuntary contribution to the educational, religious, or charitable causes granted exemptions from liability, the copyright owner is permitted by law to veto performance of his or her work by serving notice on the person responsible for a particular performance at least seven days before the date of the performance, along with a statement of the reasons for objecting to the performance.

Secondary Transmissions. Certain enumerated *secondary transmissions* ("the further transmitting of a primary transmission simultaneously with the primary transmission") are exempted from liability for copyright infringement. The types of secondary transmissions of copyrighted materials that do not produce liability for infringement are specified in intricate detail.

Secondary transmissions made by the management of a hotel or apartment house are exempt. For example, the owner of an apartment house may install a single television antenna that transmits television signals to all apartments in the apartment house. To qualify for the exemption, management must transmit broadcast signals in their entirety, without deleting or adding advertising or making any other change in the signal as received. The apartment house or hotel must be located in the local service area of the broadcasting station; transmission must take place only to "private lodgings" of guests or tenants; and no direct charge may be made for the secondary transmission.

Cable television systems are subject to a compulsory license; that is, they can obtain a license for retransmission of copyrighted broadcast signals without direct negotiations with the owner of copyright in the broadcast. Retransmission of television signals by a cable system is a secondary transmission. A cable system desiring to qualify for the compulsory license must record a notice of its claim of compulsory license with the Copyright Office. The compulsory license subjects the cable system to a compulsory royalty specified by statute in an amount based on the cable system's level of gross receipts. Royalties are paid to the Copyright Royalty Tribunal, which distributes each year's receipts in response to claims filed by copyright owners. As a general matter, the compulsory license permits cable systems to make only simultaneous transmissions of primary transmissions. A delayed secondary transmission of a primary transmission is permitted only if certain conditions are met: the nonsimultaneous secondary transmission occurs only once; the cable system does not delete or edit the original transmission; and the videotape of the original transmission is not further copied and is erased at some time during the calendar quarter in which the taping occurs.

Ephemeral Recordings. There are specific exemptions from liability for copying in situations where the user of a copyrighted work under license is permitted to make ephemeral copies (not meant to be retained permanently by the copier) of the work under circumstances outlined in detail in the copyright law.

One exemption for ephemeral recordings applies to a "transmitting organization entitled to transmit to the public a performance or display of a work, under a license or transfer of the copyright." The term *transmitting organization* has been interpreted to mean radio and television broadcasters and other transmitters of copyrighted works, like cable television services. The ephemeral recording exception for transmitting organizations does not apply to motion pictures or other audiovisual works. The transmitting organization is permitted to make no more than one copy, and that copy must be retained and used only by the transmitting organization making the copy. The copying must be for use in connection with the transmitting organization's transmissions within its own local service area or for the transmitting organization's archives. Unless used for archival purposes, the copy must be destroyed within six months from the date of transmission to the public. If permitted to do so by the grant of license that permitted the original transmission by the transmitting organization, the transmitting organization may make additional transmissions of the copy during the six-month period following the date of first transmission.

Instructional broadcasters and other educational groups may, without liability for infringement, make up to thirty copies of a copyrighted work that may be exchanged with other similar organizations. This right is conditioned on no additional copies being made from the thirty copies produced under the exemption. One copy may be made for archival purposes, but all other copies must be destroyed within seven years from the date of first transmission of the copyrighted work to the public.

Churches, nonprofit organizations, and governmental bodies are permitted to make copies of transmissions of works "embodying a performance of a nondramatic musical work of a religious nature, or of a sound recording of such a musical work." This exemption is subject to the conditions that no more than one copy is made for each transmitting organization; that when the organization making the copy permits its use by another, there is no charge for such use; that any recipient of such a copy makes no more than a single transmission to the public using the copy; that the recipient of a copy is authorized by the copyright owner to make a further transmission of the work; and that, except for a single archival copy, all other copies are destroyed within one year from the date of public transmission.

Noncommercial transmissions to handicapped audiences are exempted from liability for infringement. The maker of such a transmission is permitted to make no more than ten ephemeral copies of the work so long as any such copy is retained and used only by the organization making the copy, no additional copies of any such copy are made, any such copy is used only for transmissions to handicapped audiences or for archival purposes, and an organization using any such copy does not levy any charge for its use.

> Peter, a seventy-year-old artist who shuns all publicity, is finally prevailed upon to permit an exhibition of his paintings at a museum. To promote the exhibition the museum, with Peter's consent, prints postcards bearing several of Peter's paintings to be mailed to members of the public in the area. In a news story about the exhibition, a television station depicts the postcards on its evening news program. Peter registers a violent complaint, and threatens legal action for infringement of the copyrights protecting his paintings. Why is the station unworried?

Pictorial, Graphic, and Sculptural Works. It is not infringement of the copyright in a pictorial, graphic, or sculptural work that has been reproduced in a "useful article" to produce, distribute, or display pictures or photographs of the useful article in connection with advertisements or commentaries relating to the distribution or display of the useful article or in connection with news reports. Thus a television news program does not infringe the copyright in a copyrighted comic strip by photographing a toy item bearing the likeness of a character from the strip or broadcasting a picture of the toy item in connection with a news report about the toy item.

Sound Recordings. A sound recording (phonograph record, audio tape, or compact disc embodying a musical performance) is subject to copyright protection independent of the musical compositions embodied in it. The performance of the music by the artist or artists making the recording is entitled to copyright protection separate and distinct from the copyrights on the musical compositions performed. However, the owner of copyright in a sound recording possesses only the right to duplication of the sound recording in forms that "directly or indirectly recapture the actual sounds fixed in the recording." If a sound recording reproduces, for example, twelve songs in a particular order, the copyright owner would not have the right to prevent the making or sale of another sound recording reproducing the same twelve songs in the same order, so long as the second maker recorded the songs independently. A copier of the actual sounds contained in the sound recording would be liable to the sound recording's copyright owner for infringement.

Compulsory License: Musical Works. Once a musical work is distributed to the public in the United States in the form of a sound recording, that work becomes subject to compulsory license provisions of the copyright law. The compulsory license permits the person obtaining the license to reproduce the copyrighted musical work in the form of phonorecords. A compulsory license may be obtained only by a person whose primary purpose in making phonorecords is to distribute them to the public for private use. The person obtaining a compulsory license may make an arrangement of the work to the extent required to accommodate the specific type of performance included in a phonorecord, but the arrangement may not modify the melody or fundamental character of the work.

A person desiring a compulsory license must serve on the owner of copyright in the musical work a notice of intention to obtain a compulsory license. The notice must be served within thirty days after the making of a phonorecord incorporating the work and before any of the phonorecords are distributed to the public. The notice must comply and be served in accordance with requirements established by the Copyright Office. If notice is not filed and served in accordance with the statute, absent a license negotiated directly with the copyright owner, producing a phonorecord containing a copyrighted musical work would be an infringement of copyright in the work.

In order to receive royalty payments under a compulsory license, the owner of copyright in a musical work must be identified in the records of the Copyright Office as the owner. The royalty payable under the compulsory license is fixed by statute and depends on the amount of playing time allotted to the copyrighted work in a particular phonorecord. Royalty payments and accountings must be made within twenty days of the end of each calendar month and comply with the Copyright Office regulations governing such accountings.

Compulsory License: Jukeboxes. The Berne Act eliminated the need for jukebox operators to obtain compulsory licenses because such licenses were viewed as being inconsistent with adherence to the Berne Convention. The Berne Act substituted for the jukebox compulsory license a voluntary license agreement program that the jukebox industry has indicated it finds acceptable. Under the copyright law before its amendment by the Berne Act, the operator of a "coin-operated phonorecord player" (in other words, a jukebox) was permitted to play copyrighted music on his or her machine only after obtaining a compulsory license from the Copyright Office.

> Kitty is perturbed by the unauthorized display of one of her comic strips on the evening news show on her local public broadcasting station. The station manager tells Kitty that he feels the station has no obligation to compensate her for its use of her strip. Why is his position correct?

Noncommercial Broadcasting. Noncommercial educational broadcast stations are entitled to a compulsory license for use of two categories of works: published nondramatic musical works and published pictorial, graphic, and sculptural works. The owners of copyrights in these types of works are entitled to appoint common agents to negotiate and receive payments for use of their works by noncommercial broadcasters.

Subject to the terms of any voluntary license agreements, noncommercial broadcasters are entitled to perform or display published nondramatic musical works or published pictorial, graphic, and sculptural works in the course of public transmissions. They may also produce a program for transmission incorporating published nondramatic musical works and published pictorial, graphic, and sculptural works, so long as the production is made by a nonprofit institution only for the purpose of noncommercial transmission. A governmental body or nonprofit institution may make copies of a transmission program made by a noncommercial broadcaster so long as the copy is made simultaneously with transmission, but the copy may be used only in connection with face-to-face teaching activities in a nonprofit institution within seven days after initial transmission, and the copy must be destroyed at the end of that period. The statute makes it clear that the noncommercial broadcasting exemption applies only to the specific types of works mentioned in the statute and does not apply to types of works not specifically mentioned, such as nondramatic literary works or dramatic musical works.

Performing Rights Societies

One of the rights granted to the owner of copyright in a musical composition is the exclusive right to perform the work. Such a copyright owner would encounter immense difficulties attempting to police his or her performance right. There are thousands of potential users around the country for a musical composition—radio and television stations, nightclubs, theaters, and so on. Conversely, it would be extremely difficult for users of the performance right in copyrighted musical works to negotiate directly with the owners of copyright in each musical work prior to using that work. A radio station, for example, might find itself using in the course of a broadcast day some 250 musical works, the copyrights on all of which might have different owners.

These difficulties are overcome by performing rights societies. The most important of the U.S. performing rights societies are the American Society of Composers, Authors and Publishers (ASCAP) and Broadcast Music, Inc. (BMI). Also of importance is SESAC, Inc., the name of which is an acronym for the Society of European Stage Authors and Composers. Owners of copyright in musical works transfer their performance rights and the right to pursue infringements of their copyrighted

---

Barney, owner of a country-style bar in a remote area of eastern Tennessee, hires different bands to perform bluegrass music in the bar every Saturday night. The bands invariably perform copyrighted tunes from the current top-twenty list of country music. Barney is vaguely aware that some sort of permission may be necessary to permit the performance of copyrighted music in his bar, but he thinks "How will the owner of copyright in a single song find out a band has been performing the song in my bar?" How can Barney come to regret his remark?

works to one of the performing rights societies. Users of copyrighted musical material may then contact the performing rights society and obtain either a blanket license covering all copyrighted works represented by that society or one permitting use of copyrighted musical works on a per-program basis. Thus, a radio station with an ASCAP blanket license is entitled to broadcast all copyrighted musical works represented by ASCAP. The performing rights society license will obligate the licensee to pay a royalty to the performing rights society, which then distributes the amounts collected to the music copyright owners, calculating each owner's share on the basis of a formula derived by monitoring use of copyrighted works by licensee stations.

The operator of an establishment in which copyrighted music is performed is responsible for obtaining the necessary performing rights society license. If a nightclub owner hires a live band to perform for his customers, he cannot assume that the band has obtained the necessary license for performance of copyrighted musical works. Without such a license, the nightclub owner will be liable for copyright infringement as a result of performance of copyrighted songs. The performing rights societies, as part of the service performed for the copyright owners they represent, conduct random investigations of establishments where copyrighted music is performed and are aggressive in pursuing the owners of establishments who have not bothered to obtain licenses.

Although obtaining a license from one of the performing rights societies is the most expeditious means of acquiring the right to perform a copyrighted musical work, the copyright user is also entitled to negotiate a license directly with the copyright owner.

Chain of Liability; Vicarious Liability for Reproducing Infringing Work of Another

In many cases of copyright infringement, more than one party or entity may be liable to the copyright owner for infringe-

> Renée notes that character merchandise jewelry is a hot seller in her gift shop. She finds, however, that it is relatively expensive compared to similar jewelry not using characters; for that reason her profit margin is not as good as it could be. Renée believes she has made a real coup when a salesman sells her, for about half the amount she usually pays, character jewelry made in Taiwan. She receives a letter from lawyers representing the owner of the copyrights on the character, indicating the Taiwan-origin jewelry is unauthorized and infringing. Renée thinks "I didn't know it was infringing, so what can they do to me?" She throws the letter away. Why does she subsequently conclude that she should have responded to the letter and cooperated with the lawyers?

ment. The act of copying without permission is the original infringement. Lack of knowledge on the part of subsequent sellers or users that the original copier copied is not a defense to an action for infringement. In a situation where an infringer copies a copyrighted magazine article and submits his infringing work to a publisher for inclusion in an anthology, all of the following could be liable to the copyright owner for infringement:

- The infringer who initially makes the copies of the copyrighted article
- The publishing company that assembles and distributes the anthology
- The printer who prints the anthology for the publishing company.
- The retail store that puts into distribution copies of the anthology

The copying, performance, or distribution of an infringing work may result in liability for infringement even if the person committing the infringing act is unaware he or she is dealing with an infringing work.

Vicarious liability for copyright infringement results when one person is held liable for infringement as a result of infringing acts by another. A corporate officer who supervises infringing activities by his corporation will be liable, along with the corporation, for infringement. The owner of a nightclub where musicians present infringing performances of copyrighted musical works will be liable for infringement even though he did not participate directly in the performances. In order for vicarious liability to be imposed, the vicarious infringer must control the activities of the person who actually commits the infringing act.

Consequences of Infringement

When there is any doubt whether use of material produced by others will infringe copyright in the material, the wise course is to consult with counsel. Any doubt should be resolved by obtaining from the copyright owner a license or permission to reproduce the material. The consequences of making an erroneous decision and as a result being held liable for infringement are numerous. The infringer may find himself subject to the following penalties:

- Temporary or permanent injunction against continued distribution of infringing material
- Delivery to the court and destruction of all infringing copies
- An accounting to the copyright owner for actual damages caused by the infringing activity and any profits earned from the infringing activity
- As an alternative to actual damages and profits, statutory damages, which may be set as high as $20,000 ($10,000 prior to the effective date of the Berne Act) per infringement, at the court's discretion

- Reimbursing the plaintiff copyright owner for the owner's attorneys' fees
- Reimbursement of the plaintiff's costs

Where an infringement is found to be willful, the statutory civil damages may be increased to a maximum of $100,000 ($50,000 prior to the effective date of the Berne Act) per infringement, at the discretion of the court; there may also be criminal liability for willful infringement. When the harsh consequences of being found guilty of infringement are considered, it almost always makes sense to remove any doubt by obtaining from the copyright owner permission to make the desired use of the copyrighted work.

CHAPTER 4

PROTECTION OF MEDIA-OWNED TRADEMARKS AND SERVICE MARKS

Types of Marks Protected

Publishers, broadcasters, and journalists use many names, phrases, and symbols that function as trademarks or service marks and are entitled to protection as such. Among these are:

- **Periodical titles.** Titles of newspapers, magazines, and other periodicals function as trademarks. Examples of periodical titles qualifying for trademark protection include THE NEW YORK TIMES; NEWSWEEK; CONGRESSIONAL QUARTERLY; VOGUE.
- **Titles of syndicated materials.** Titles of syndicated materials such as columns, comic strips, and puzzle features serve as trademarks. Examples are MISS MANNERS and BEETLE BAILEY.
- **Slogans.** Advertising slogans function as service marks. For example, the slogan WE PLAY HITS would function as a service mark for radio broadcasting services.

- **Call letters.** Call letters of radio and television stations function as service marks. Since the Federal Communication Commission no longer regulates the selection of call letters, registering them as service marks is advisable.
- **Program titles.** Titles of radio and television programs (for example, THE PRAIRIE HOME COMPANION; THE MCNEIL/LEHRER NEWS HOUR, and FAMILY TIES) are service marks.
- **Imprints.** Imprints used by publishers (for example, BANTAM and PENGUIN) are trademarks.

Rights Created by Use; Priority; Intent to Use Filings Under 1988 Trademark Act

> Pete, the promotional director for a Dallas radio station, decides to go head-to-head with another station in the Dallas market using the same format by adopting one of his competitor's advertising slogans. He has a trademark search conducted and finds that the competitor has not registered or applied to register the slogan either federally or with the Texas secretary of state. "Fine," says Pete, "they've slipped up. Without a registration, they're unprotected, and I'm free to use the slogan myself." Pete prints 50,000 bumper stickers using the slogan and promotes it heavily on the air. Why is Pete in for a shock?

The 1988 Trademark Act introduced into the Lanham Act, which provides for federal protection of trademarks, a significant alternative to the traditional practice of establishing rights by use. The Lanham Act continues to permit applications for federal registration of marks based on actual use, but it is now possible to apply for federal registration of a trademark or service mark on the basis of a bona fide intention to use. While for unregistered marks the traditional first-use priority will continue to apply, it is now possible to acquire trademark rights under the Lanham Act without use of the mark. (See page 54, for details of applying for trademark rights prior to use.)

Until the effective date of the 1988 Trademark Act (November 16, 1989), the general rule in the United States, unlike many foreign countries, was that trademark and service mark rights were created only by use of a mark. From the moment a magazine publisher commenced distribution of copies of his magazine, he or she possessed trademark rights in the magazine's title. The prior user in a particular geographic area possessed priority rights over a subsequent user of the same mark in connection with identical or similar goods or services in the same geographic area. Except where a federal trademark or service mark registration had been issued (see below), the prior user of a mark had no rights against even a subsequent user of the mark in remote areas. For example, the user of an advertising slogan not federally registered in a geographic area limited to New England would not have any right to prevent use by another of the same advertising slogan in connection with the same services in California, even if the California user began using the mark later than the first use by the New England user.

Selection of New Marks

Selection of a new trademark or service mark can be an extremely important decision. The name under which a product or service is advertised and sold may have an enormous impact on its success or failure.

Strong and Weak Marks. Selection of a mark that in some fashion conveys to consumers some of the characteristics of the product is a frequent tendency. The baker marketing a new type of bread might wish to call it DELICIOUS (or DEE-LICIOUS, or DEE-LISHUS, or some other variant spelling of the descriptive term). Terms that describe the characteristics of the product or service being sold are termed *weak* trademarks, not entitled to a wide scope of protection. The most valuable types of trademarks, considered *strong* and entitled to extensive protection, are coined or arbitrary marks with nothing whatsoever to do with the product or services in connection with which they are used (examples EXXON and KODAK). It is also possible for a common word to become a strong mark because it is used as a trademark on a product that has no association with the mark (MARATHON for gasoline, APPLE for computers).

In addition to descriptive marks, several other types of commonly used marks are not considered strong. Among these are surnames, geographic terms, and foreign-language translations of descriptive or generic English words. However, in each of these cases trademark or servicemark protection may eventually become available through the mark's acquiring *distinctiveness* or *secondary meaning* if the mark, through lengthy use or a significant advertising campaign, becomes widely associated in the minds of the public with the user's product or services. GARFIELD, a surname, is widely recognized as a trademark for a syndicated comic strip, plush toys, and dozens of other products. STRIDE-RITE, while descriptive of footwear, is a well-known and heavily promoted mark entitled to significant degrees of protection.

Generic Terms. It is not possible to obtain trademark protection for generic terms, even through the acquisition of secondary meaning. A *generic term* is the everyday word by which a particular product or service is denoted. In the example used earlier, DELICIOUS is the trademark (albeit a descriptive one), and *bread* is the generic term for the product. In some cases, words that started out as arbitrary coined trademarks have become through usage generic terms for the products on which the marks were used. ASPIRIN and CELLOPHANE were at one time trademarks for an over-the-counter pain remedy and a clear material used for wrapping food. A trademark owner finding his or her mark in danger of becoming a generic term through public use may wage an expensive advertising campaign emphasizing that the mark should not be used as a generic term and implement a policy of sending notifications to those who misuse the mark.

> Alex is retained to modernize the image of a New York publishing house. A key facet of Alex's program involves the publisher's launching of a new line of books under the DYNAMIC imprint. Several hundred thousand dollars are expended in print and television advertising commitments for the DYNAMIC line of books. Four new titles are printed bearing the DYNAMIC mark. Three days after the first ad for DYNAMIC books appears in *Publisher's Weekly,* Alex's publisher client receives a letter from a small California publisher that indicates the California company has published books under the DYNAMIC trademark since 1956; enclosed with the letter is a copy of a federal trademark registration certificate for the mark in the name of the California publisher. Why does Alex face a serious problem?

Trademark Searches. Any time use of a new trademark or service mark is contemplated, it is advisable to conduct a trademark search. Several companies offer several different types of search, tailored to the particular circumstances surrounding the launch of a product line or service utilizing a new mark. At the very minimum, a search of the federal trademark registries and state trademark registries should be conducted. Also advisable is a common-law search, which search services can conduct in trade and telephone directories as well as other sources that list unregistered trademark uses and names. It is now possible to conduct an immediate preliminary search of the federal and state trademark registries using a computer database available to customers of LEXIS, a computer legal-research service sub-scribed to by many law firms. The only information needed to commence a search is the intended mark and the relevant product or services.

Federal Registration of Marks

While use of a trademark or service mark creates rights in the mark, the protection available to a mark can be significantly increased by obtaining registration of the mark on one of the registers of the U.S. Patent and Trademark Office. The registration process is commenced by filing a federal trademark or service mark application with the Trademark Office.

Registration Based on Use of Mark in Commerce. A trademark or service mark is eligible for federal registration if in use in interstate commerce. To support a federal trademark application based on actual use, a mark must be used on actual products or on related packaging materials (for example, boxes or hangtags) in connection with a shipment of the goods from one state to another. In the case of a service mark, use in interstate commerce may take place through use of the mark on advertising material. For example, publication of an advertisement using the service mark in a publication having interstate circulation will serve as a basis for filing a federal service mark application.

Token Use. Prior to the effective date of the 1988 Trademark Act, many users of new marks sought to create a basis for filing a federal application as early as possible by making a so-called *token use* of the mark. This involved making up a small shipment of products bearing the mark and shipping them to a customer in another state. At the same time it made filing a trademark application on the basis of intent to use possible, the 1988 Trademark Act eliminated token use as a basis for a federal trademark filing.

> Del decides that he can make a million dollars selling bag-pipe music on compact discs under the HAGGIS label. Before beginning to market his product, he wants to make sure his use of the HAGGIS name is protected. How can he accomplish this?

Application Based on Intent to Use. As discussed on page 49, the Trademark Act of 1988 now provides the trademark owner with two alternative bases for seeking federal protection for his or her mark. The traditional federal application based on actual use of the mark in interstate commerce remains available, but a federal application may now be filed on the basis of intent to use.

> To accompany a federal service mark application for his station's new advertising slogan, Myron provides his trademark counsel with one advertising flyer, one bumper sticker, one newspaper ad, one magazine ad, and one game card. Why do these items not fulfill Trademark Office requirements as to specimens?

Federal Application Based on Actual Use. Federal trademark and service mark applications are filed using forms specified by the regulations of the Trademark Office. An application based on actual use of the mark will contain the name and address of the user, identify the mark for which registration is sought, indicate the types of goods or services in connection with which the mark is used, and set forth the dates of first use of the mark and first use in interstate commerce. The application must be executed by the applicant—or, in the case of a corporation, an officer of the corporation. The person executing the application confirms under oath that the contents of the application are true. If an applicant seeks to register a mark in a distinctive form (as opposed to registration of the mark in block letters), the application must contain a special drawing of the mark in conformity with the rules of the Trademark Office. When submitted to the Trademark Office, the application must be accompanied by five identical specimens showing the mark as actually used (such as five identical hangtags for a trademark or five copies of a single magazine advertisement for a service mark).

Contents of Federal Application Based on Intent to Use. An application for federal registration of a mark based on intent to use differs from an application based on actual use in the following respects. No use dates need be included, and no specimens showing use of the mark are required. Rather than swearing that the mark covered by the application is in use, the applicant must swear to a "bona fide intention, under circumstances showing the good faith" of the applicant to use the mark in commerce (that is, in the ordinary course of trade, and not for purposes of reserving the mark).

Classification of Marks. Trademarks and service marks are registered according to a classification system that groups merchandise items and services having similar characteristics in single classes. The United States now uses the international classification system derived from the classification system of the United Kingdom. The international classification system consists of thirty-four classes for products (Classes 1 through 34) and eight classes for services (Classes 35 through 42). A listing of the international trademark and service mark classes as they appear in the regulations of the Trademark Office is contained in Appendix D.

The classification system is important for registration purposes because the application must identify the goods or services in connection with which a mark is used (or intended to be used), broken down by classes; the application fee specified by statute (currently $175) must be paid for each class for which registration is sought. A trademark user wishing to register his or her mark as it is used or intended to be used on, for example, both T-shirts and toy items would need to file a single application covering both Classes 25 and 28 or two separate applications for the two classes. In either case it would be necessary to pay a $175 application fee for each class.

Principal and Supplemental Registers. An application must specify on which of the two registers established by the Lanham Act the applicant desires the registration ultimately issuing from the application to be lodged. The Lanham Act establishes a Principal Register and a Supplemental Register. The Principal Register is the more desirable of the two, with the Supplemental Register being reserved for descriptive terms, surnames, and other marks for one reason or another not registrable on the Principal Register. An application for registration on the Supplemental Register must be based on use, and may not be based on intention to use.

Application Examination. Each trademark application is subject to an examination conducted by attorney examiners employed by the Trademark Office. The examiners ensure that each application contains all necessary information and, where actual use is alleged, is consistent with accompanying appropriate specimens showing use of the mark to be registered. For example, an examiner may raise a question if the individual executing an application on behalf of a corporation is described by a title, like general manager, not typically the title of a corporate officer. If the specimens accompanying an application alleging actual use bear a name other than the name of the applicant, the examiner will query the relationship between the applicant and the other named entity.

In addition to examining the application for appropriate form and content, the examiner is required by statute to reject applications for marks that violate one or more of several different statutory prohibitions. The Trademark Office is not permitted

> Silas Smith, a publishing entrepreneur well known for the
> high opinion he holds of himself, launches a monthly
> magazine entitled *Smith*. He decides to seek federal trade-
> mark protection for the magazine title and files a federal
> trademark application. Why does the application encoun-
> ter difficulties in the Trademark Office?

to issue registrations for marks confusingly similar with marks
already registered. A mark that is merely descriptive or is primarily a surname is not entitled to registration on the Principal
Register unless the applicant is able to convince the examiner
that the mark has acquired distinctiveness or secondary meaning (in other words, has become generally known to members
of the public). Primarily geographically descriptive or decep-
tively misdescriptive marks are similarly not registrable unless
distinctiveness is shown. Further, the following types of mark
are identified by statute as ineligible for registration whether or
not distinctiveness can be shown:

- Marks containing deceptive matter or immoral or scandal-
  ous matter; marks that disparage or falsely suggest a connection with persons (living or dead), institutions, beliefs,
  or national symbols or bring them into contempt or
  disrepute
- The flag or coat of arms or other insignia of the United
  States, any state or municipality, or any foreign country
- The name, portrait, or signature of a living individual, except with written consent, or the name, signature, or portrait of a deceased U.S. president during the life of his widow, except with the widow's written consent

Objections to an application, whether requiring technical ad-
justments or clarifications from the applicant or raising one of
the statutory bars to registration, are contained in a communi-

cation from the Trademark Office called an *Office Action*. The applicant has six months from the date of an Office Action to file an appropriate response; otherwise the application is considered abandoned. Responses to Office Actions must respond to all points raised by the examiner. When an Office Action raises legal issues, the response may contain legal arguments and cite cases as in a legal brief to a court. If the examiner takes the position that a mark is confusingly similar with one already registered, the applicant may in response submit legal arguments to the effect that the mark for which registration is sought is not confusingly similar with the one cited by the examiner on the ground, for example, that the goods covered by the cited registration are different from those on which the applicant uses his or her mark. If the examiner has raised a "merely descriptive" or "surname" objection, the applicant is entitled to place before the examiner, in an affidavit, evidence that the mark has become distinctive through widespread advertising or widespread sales of products bearing the mark or through more than five years of continuous use.

Publication for Opposition. If the applicant is able to deal satisfactorily with any issues raised, the examiner will approve the application. If the application is based on actual use, the mark will then be "published for opposition" in the weekly *Official Gazette* published by the Trademark Office. Once a mark is published for opposition, anyone who feels he or she would be damaged by registration of the mark has a thirty-day period following the date of publication to file an opposition to registration. An opposition proceeding is commenced by filing a Notice of Opposition, similar to a complaint in a civil lawsuit, setting forth the grounds for the opposition. The applicant is permitted to file an answer; an opposition proceeding, which is tried before the Trademark Trial and Appeal Board (TTAB), has many of the characteristics of civil litigation.

If an application based on intent to use is approved, the applicant will be issued a notice of allowance. The applicant then has six months from the date of the notice to make the required bona fide use of the mark in commerce and to submit to the Trademark Office specimens showing that use. This six-month period can be extended for further six-month periods (to a maximum of twenty-four months) by the applicant's filing of a verified statement of the applicant's continuing intention to use the mark, demonstrating "good cause" for the requested extension, and paying an additional fee. Once the applicant files acceptable evidence of use with the Trademark Office, the application will be published for opposition, in the same fashion as an actual use application.

Examiner's Rejection of Application. If the applicant is unable to satisfy the examiner that his or her mark is entitled to registration, two responses are possible. The application can be abandoned (by not responding to an outstanding Office Action during the six-month period following the date of the action) or an appeal of the decision can be made to the TTAB.

Length of Protection. If no opposition is filed to registration of a mark during the thirty-day period following its publication in the *Official Gazette,* the applicant is issued a federal trademark registration approximately three months following the date of publication. A federal registration issued before November 16, 1989, the effective date of the Trademark Act of 1988, is valid for a period of twenty years from the date of registration. The Trademark Act of 1988 reduced the term for a federal registration to ten years. In order to remove registrations for unused marks from the Trademark Office registers, registrants are required, during the one-year period following the fifth anniversary of issuance of the registration, to file an affidavit stating that the mark covered by the registration is still being used by the registrant in interstate commerce. If the affidavit of use is not filed, the registration is canceled as of the sixth anniversary of its issuance. Registrations not canceled for failure to file a required use affidavit may continue to be renewed for additional ten-year renewal periods for as long as the registrant continues to use the mark.

Amendment to Supplemental Register. If an application based on use is rejected on certain grounds—for example, that a mark is primarily a surname—the applicant is entitled to amend his or her initial Principal Register application to request registration on the Supplemental Register. Prior to the effective date of the Trademark Act of 1988, this procedure was available only if the mark had been in use for a minimum of one year preceding the date of amendment to the Supplemental Register. This one-year use requirement was eliminated by the Trademark Act of 1988; however, actual use is still required.

Filing for Supplemental Register Registration. It is permissible initially to file for registration on the Supplemental rather than the Principal Register. Under prior law, such filing required one year of use of the mark prior to filing, a requirement eliminated by the Trademark Act of 1988. As a practical matter, there is no reason to file initially for a Supplemental Register registration because of the ease of amending a Principal Register registration to make it a Supplemental Register registration. A Supplemental Register registration is not subject to opposition proceedings, although it may be attacked through cancellation proceedings.

Cancellation of Registration. Anyone who misses an opportunity to file an opposition proceeding is nevertheless entitled to file with the TTAB a proceeding seeking cancellation of a registration. The federal district courts are also empowered to cancel federal registrations at issue in civil litigation before them at the request of a party to the litigation showing appropriate grounds for cancellation.

Benefits of Federal Registration

The owner of a federal trademark or service mark registration on the Principal Register acquires a number of significant and important benefits under the provisions of the Lanham Act.

(Many of these benefits do not apply to Supplemental Register registrations.)

Registered Trademark Symbol. The registrant is entitled to use the registered trademark symbol ® in connection with the registered trademark or service mark, which may have a deterrent effect on potential infringers. Use of the symbol is not mandatory, although certain remedies against infringers may be lost if the symbol is not used. Note that the frequently used notations "TM" and "SM" have no legal significance, but merely reflect the user's interest in claiming trademark or service mark protection for the mark bearing the notation.

Suit in Federal Court. The registrant is entitled to enforce his or her trademark or service mark rights in federal courts rather than state courts.

Prima Facie Evidence. A federal registration is prima facie evidence, in a court proceeding or Trademark Office proceeding involving the mark, of the validity of the registration, the registrant's ownership of the mark, and the exclusive right of the registrant to use the mark in commerce. Anyone attacking the validity of the registration or the mark covered by the registration bears the burden of overcoming the rebuttable presumptions created by the prima facie evidence rule.

Damages and Attorneys' Fees. The Lanham Act specifies that the infringer of a registered trademark must pay to the registrant the infringer's profits, any damages sustained by the registrant, and the costs incurred by the registrant in bringing the infringement action. At its discretion, the federal court trying a case involving infringement of a registered mark may award damages up to three times the amount of actual damages proved by the registrant. In "exceptional cases" the court may award reasonable attorneys' fees to the prevailing party. In the case of an intentional infringement involving use of a "counterfeit" mark (defined as a counterfeit of a mark registered on the

Trademark Office Principal Register), the court is required, unless it finds extenuating circumstances, to award the registrant judgment for three times any profits or damages shown, whichever is greater, together with reasonable attorneys' fees.

Actual and Constructive Notice. A federal trademark or servicemark registration places the registrant's claim of rights in his mark in the records of the Trademark Office. A person considering using a confusingly similar mark who conducts a trademark search will acquire actual knowledge of the registration.

> Mark develops a slogan to be used by seventeen radio stations owned by his employer, all east of the Mississippi River. He has a trademark search conducted and notes that a station in Oregon has already obtained a federal servicemark registration for the same slogan. Further investigation reveals that the station owning the registration is the only one operated by its owner, and that it advertises only in Oregon and California. Mark decides that since the owner of the registration is so remote there will not be any conflict, and proceeds to introduce the slogan in all seventeen of his company's markets. The Oregon station is purchased by Megalomania Broadcasting, which likes the slogan so much that it decides to use it on all forty of its stations throughout the country. Why does Mark now find himself in an embarrassing position?

Even more important, a federal registration has the effect of placing people throughout the United States on constructive notice that the registrant claims exclusive rights in the mark. Prior to the effective date of the Trademark Act of 1988, this constructive notice effect commenced from the date of issuance of the registration. Under the Trademark Act of 1988, however, the constructive notice effect of a federal registration commences from the date of the filing of the application (if the application ultimately matures into a registration).

A federal registration on the Principal Register does not give the registrant the right to prevent others from using the mark in geographic areas in which the registrant is not using the mark. However, by virtue of the registration's constructive notice effect, the registrant possesses a reserved right to expand use of his or her registered mark into remote geographic areas, and, once that expansion occurs, to prevent use of the registered mark by others who began using the mark after the date of registration. For example, a registrant may have obtained federal registration of his or her mark on the basis of use of the mark on products in interstate commerce between only two states, New York and New Jersey. If another person begins using the same mark on the same products in Oregon after the date of registration, the registrant would have no right to prevent that use so long as use of his or her mark is limited to New Jersey and New York. However, once the registrant expands his or her operation so that he or she is selling goods bearing the mark in Oregon, he or she is entitled to an injunction against use of the mark by the other person, even if the other person has used the mark in Oregon for many years.

The constructive notice effect of a federal registration may well deter a potential user of a mark even in a remote geographic area, since it could prove foolish to spend money and time developing goodwill in a mark, the use of which could be blocked at any time by the holder of a federal registration who is expanding use of his or her registered mark.

The constructive notice effect of a federal registration has no applicability to trademark uses in existence prior to the effective date of constructive notice (the date of registration for one issued prior to November 16, 1989, or the date of application for a registration issued on a filing after November 16, 1989). The issuance of a federal registration has the effect, however, of freezing prior users' rights in the geographic areas where they used a mark at the time the registration was issued. To return to the example of the registrant who obtained registration on the basis of use between New York and New Jersey, if the Oregon user commenced use of the mark prior to the constructive notice date of the registrant's registration, the Oregon user would have a continuing right to use the mark in Oregon and, in fact, to prevent the registrant from using the mark in Oregon. However, the Oregon user's rights would be frozen in the precise geographic area where his or her mark was being used at the effective date of constructive notice resulting from the registration. By virtue of the constructive notice effect of his or her federal registration, the registrant would possess the right to enjoin use of the mark in areas into which the Oregon user might expand after the effective date of constructive notice of the registrant's registration.

State Registration of Trademarks and Service Marks

Each of the fifty states has enacted a statute for the protection of trademarks and service marks on a statewide basis. State trademark and service mark registration statutes vary widely in their provisions, so it is impossible to discuss all of them here. A state registration is typically less expensive and quicker to obtain than a federal registration.

State trademark statutes often provide the owner of a registered mark the same types of remedies available to a federal registrant, including provisions permitting state courts to award state trademark registrants an infringer's profits, damages proved by the registrant, and injunctive relief.

A state trademark or service mark registration is not likely to receive the same respect from a court or from a potential infringer that would be given a federal registration, because the state governmental agencies responsible for issuing state registrations (frequently the office of the state secretary of state) in most cases do not conduct any substantive review of applications with the objective of rejecting registration of, for example, descriptive marks or surnames. Issuance of a state registration for a mark usually indicates only that there were no confusingly similar marks, trade names, or corporate names already registered with the secretary of state. Further, a state registration has effect only within the boundaries of the state, so it cannot be asserted against users outside the state even when use occurs in areas in close proximity to the state of the registrant.

When someone seeking protection for a trademark or service mark is using the mark in interstate commerce, it makes sense in virtually all cases to seek federal registration of the mark. When there is use in interstate commerce, a state registration should be sought in states of commercial interest to the trademark user only to provide interim protection during the lengthy period required for obtaining a federal registration.

Assignment of Marks

Trademarks and trademark registrations may be assigned like other kinds of property. To be valid, a trademark assignment must convey not only the mark but also the goodwill of the business in connection with which the mark is used. Assignments of federal registrations should be recorded with the Trademark Office. Assignments of state registrations should be recorded with the relevant agency of the state government that issued the registration.

Foreign Protection of Trademarks and Service Marks

Foreign Registration. In contrast to copyrights, with foreign protection often available to the U.S. copyright proprietor without the necessity of any special action, trademark protec-

Platypus Publishing's *Platypus* magazine starts as a small quarterly and grows into a monthly with substantial circulation. Platypus owns a U.S. federal registration for the PLATYPUS mark. Platypus decides to produce an international edition for distribution in South America. With the title protected in the United States, Platypus feels that nothing else need be done. However, an individual named Pablo registered PLATYPUS in Bolivia, in the trademark class covering publications, six months after the magazine was launched in the United States. Pablo is willing to transfer his registration to Platypus for $500,000. What could Platypus have done to avoid this?

tion is almost exclusively regional. United States trademark rights, even if the mark is registered in the U.S., are of no consequence in a foreign country. Any U.S. trademark owner who believes his trademark has potential for exploitation in foreign countries should make sure that a registration program for the mark in those countries is implemented at an early date. In many foreign countries, particularly civil law countries, there is no requirement that a mark be used prior to applying to register it. Consequently, the U.S. trademark owner can protect his mark in many foreign countries before actually using it there.

With the first person to file for registration of a mark in many foreign countries having priority rights against others, U.S. trademark owners making widespread use of a mark in the United States may find themselves unable to register or use their own marks in countries other than the United States. In many countries, entrepreneurs become trademark pirates. They monitor the U.S. media to identify marks that receive substantial publicity or are heavily advertised in the United States and which might be likely candidates for use outside the United States. Having identified a likely mark, a trademark pirate will apply to register it in his or her own country. When the U.S. trademark owner decides to expand into the trademark pirate's country, he or she is faced with the choice of either buying out the trademark pirate at an inflated price or coming up with an alternative mark to use in that country.

Trademark Surveillance. In addition to filing for foreign protection in appropriate countries at an early date, the U.S. trademark owner can also protect his or her mark by placing it under worldwide surveillance, a service offered by a number of law firms and companies. For a nominal fee, surveillance services will place designated trademarks on watch so that the trademark owner receives notification when someone else applies to register one of his or her marks in a foreign country. This will give the trademark owner an opportunity to implement opposition proceedings against the offending application. It is usually easier to prevent registration of the mark through an opposition proceeding than to file cancellation proceedings after a registration has been issued.

The Right of Publicity; Right of Non-Celebrities to Control Use of Their Names and Likenesses

The right of publicity, similar in nature to trademark/service mark rights, is the right of a celebrity to control the commercial use of his or her name and likeness. Personalities like Arnold Palmer receive substantial compensation for permitting their names and likenesses to be used for advertising all kinds of products and services. The right of publicity enables such personalities to prevent others from utilizing their names and likenesses without permission.

There have been conflicting decisions among the courts of different states on whether the right of publicity is personal to the celebrity, ceasing when the celebrity dies, or whether the right of publicity can be inherited. Thus, the commercial use of the name or likeness of a deceased celebrity could, depending

> Pascual decides to run a promotion for his television station, emphasizing print ads, billboards, and bus signs with a Bruce Springsteen "Born in the U.S.A." theme, including large photographs of Springsteen. Why may Pascual find himself faced with serious legal difficulties?

on the state where it occurs, be a violation of the right of publicity passed to the celebrity's descendants.

Non-celebrities also have the right to control commercial uses of their names and likenesses. It is good practice to obtain from individuals who appear in copyrighted works (for example, videos, ads, commericals) written releases, broadly worded to give the copyright owner the right to use the included name or image in all desired forms and media.

CHAPTER 5

ENFORCEMENT OF MEDIA TRADEMARKS AND SERVICE MARKS

Likelihood of Confusion

The objective of obtaining federal and state registrations for trademarks and service marks is to place the registrant in the most advantageous position possible to enforce his or her trademark or service mark rights when confronted with an infringer. Trademark infringement occurs when the use of a mark by one party creates likelihood of confusion with a mark owned by a prior user. Likelihood of confusion is sometimes an illusive concept that requires an analysis of a substantial number of subjective factors to reach a decision on whether confusion exists. While one case may reflect an almost 100-percent chance of a finding of likelihood of confusion (FANTASTIC used on T-shirts versus FANTASTIC used on sweatshirts), and while another case may present a 100-percent certainty of a finding of no likelihood of confusion (FANTASTIC on T-shirts versus FANTASTIC on automobiles), most cases fall somewhere within these two extremes.

In determining whether likelihood of confusion exists, the courts and the Trademark Office may examine one or more of the following points:

- Similarity of the goods (whether the goods on which the marks are used are identical or closely related)
- Similarity of the marks (whether the marks are identical or similar in spelling, pronunciation, visual appearance)
- Strength or weakness of marks (a strong mark, by virtue of being a coined or arbitrary word or as a result of widespread advertising expenditures or long periods of use, is entitled to a greater scope of protection; a weak mark, a descriptive or common word not in use for a long period of time or not widely advertised, is not entitled to a wide scope of protection)
- Channels of commerce (whether the goods on which two marks are used are marketed in the same channels of distribution to the same customers; if they are not, the likelihood of confusion is greatly reduced)
- Sophistication of customers (whether the goods or services involved are marketed to sophisticated, discriminating consumers or whether they are marketed to the public at large and, therefore, to customers less likely to notice subtle distinctions between products or services bearing similar marks)
- Similarity in advertising (whether the goods are advertised in a similar fashion or in the same media)
- Actual confusion (whether consumers have actually been confused by use of the two marks on the users' products)
- Intention of second user (whether the second user of a mark has the intention of trading on the fame and goodwill associated with the first user's mark)

All these factors may be considered in a particular decision relating to likelihood of confusion, and each may be given varying degrees of weight. There is no requirement that evidence of actual confusion (evidence that members of the public have actually been confused by two persons' use of the same or similar marks) exists for a finding of likelihood of confusion.

Enforcement of Registered Marks

If the owner of a trademark registered either federally or at the state level finds himself or herself with a case of likelihood of confusion, and if preliminary steps, such as cease-and-desist letters (letters demanding that the second user cease infringement) and negotiations with the infringing user, fail, the registrant will likely seek protection of his or her mark in the courts. The federal courts have jurisdiction over any lawsuits involving federally registered trademarks or service marks.

Remedies for Infringement of Federally Registered Marks. The owner of a federally registered mark who is able to show likelihood of confusion is entitled to one or more of the following remedies:

- Damages suffered by the trademark owner as a result of the infringing activity (may be trebled in appropriate cases at the discretion of the court)
- Profits derived by the infringer from his or her infringing acts
- Attorneys' fees (at the discretion of the court)
- Temporary and permanent injunctive relief
- Destruction of infringing products and any other materials bearing the infringing mark, including packaging, labeling, advertising materials, and the like

The Trademark Counterfeiting Act of 1984 strengthened the provisions of the Lanham Act with regard to the remedies available to trademark owners in civil cases. Where intentional trafficking is shown, the trademark owner may be entitled to an ex parte seizure (a seizure authorized by the court without prior notice to the counterfeiter) of counterfeit goods, to prevent the defendant from destroying or concealing them. It also mandates an award to the injured trademark owner, if intentional trafficking has occurred, of treble damages or treble profits, whichever is greater. Where international trafficking in counterfeit goods is proved, the trademark owner is automatically entitled to recover his or her reasonable attorneys' fees.

Remedies for Infringement of State-Registered Marks. The proprietor of a state-registered trademark or service mark who is able to show likelihood of confusion will be entitled to the remedies available under the relevant state trademark statute. State trademark laws vary from state to state, but most provide for the same types of remedies available under the Lanham Act. Naturally, a state registration may be asserted only against an infringer engaged in infringing activity in the state in which the mark is registered.

Enforcement of Unregistered Marks

Since trademark and service mark rights are created by use, it is possible for a trademark proprietor to enforce rights in an unregistered mark, under Section 43(a) of the Lanham Act (which permits the federal courts to deal with cases of unfair competition) or through actions for common law trademark infringement or unfair competition. Under the 1988 amendment to the Lanham Act, remedies available under the act for registered marks are also available to protect unregistered marks. Depending on the citizenship of the parties and the amount in controversy, actions for the protection of unregistered marks may be brought in either federal or state court.

Anti-counterfeiting Legislation

In enacting the Trademark Counterfeiting Act of 1984 (which amended the Lanham Act), Congress sought to provide trademark owners with more powerful weapons against persons involved in trademark counterfeiting—i.e., the intentional copying not only of trademarks but also of entire products. Such conduct, which seems to increase every year, costs American industry hundreds of millions of dollars and can endanger the public as well. Cheap copies of automotive and aircraft parts, drugs, and medical devices may appear identical with authorized products to the undiscerning eye but usually do not perform as well as authorized products when put to the test.

Under the Trademark Counterfeiting Act, it is a federal crime to traffic intentionally in goods and services, knowing that the goods or services are counterfeit. It is also a crime to attempt to engage in this conduct or to conspire to engage in this conduct. Individuals found guilty of violating the act are subject to up to five years imprisonment and a fine of up to $250,000. Entities other than individuals engaging in such conduct (for example, corporations) may be fined up to $1,000,000. Repeat offenders are subject to even harsher penalties.

Recording with Customs

In Taiwan Ike purchases several thousand paperback books bearing the trademark of a well-known U.S. publisher. For some reason the books are incredibly inexpensive. Ike has the books shipped to Los Angeles. Why do the books fail to clear U.S. customs?

Like a registered copyright, a federally registered trademark can be recorded with the U.S. Customs Service. The Customs Service is directed by statute to prevent the importation of goods bearing a registered trademark recorded with customs that were not produced by authority of the trademark owner.

Customs Service regulations do not require customs to exclude from the United States so-called gray-market goods—

goods bearing a trademark produced by a foreign entity having the right to use the mark in countries other than the United States. Currently opinion among the federal courts is split as to whether the sale of gray-market goods constitutes trademark infringement.

Trade Names and Corporate Names

Trade names and corporate names may be protected, even if they are not technically used as trademarks or service marks and have not been registered, on the basis of the same principles relating to infringement and unfair competition applicable to unregistered trademarks and service marks.

Liability for Infringement of Different Person Involved with Infringing Products; Vicarious Liability

It is entirely possible for others than the entity committing acts of trademark infringement to be held liable for trademark infringement and suffer the various resultant penalties. As in the case of copyright infringement, corporate officers, directors, and shareholders may be held liable for the infringing conduct of their corporation. Corporate employees may also be liable for trademark infringement. Licensees of the infringer may be guilty of infringement. Further, distributors of infringing products may also be held liable for infringement, since it is by putting the products before the public that likelihood of confusion occurs. A party who manufactures infringing products at the behest of an infringer may be liable to the trademark owner. There is provision in the law which protects innocent printers and publishers from monetary liability for printing or publishing material containing an infringing trademark or service mark. Even innocent printers and publishers may, however, be subject to injunctive relief.

CHAPTER 6

CONCLUSION

Copyrights and trademarks and service marks are types of property of particular importance to members of the media. The time to think about protecting such rights is when they first come into existence, not when an infringement situation arises. When faced with unauthorized use of his or her copyrighted work or his or her trademark, the owner who has gone to the trouble of making sure his or her protection is in order has a tremendous advantage. It is frustrating for an intellectual property attorney to be approached by a client who is extremely upset about an infringement but who has placed himself or herself in a weak position by failing to protect himself or herself properly through obtaining registrations and other required courses of conduct, before the infringement arose. Precious weeks can go by with infringing activity continuing while the protection which should have been obtained years ago is put in place. In the case of trademarks and service marks, failure to register can place a first user in the position of being unable to engage in natural expansion of his or her business, because a second user in another geographic area begins using his or her mark there or files an application based on an intent to use and acquires priority rights.

Conversely, the use of copyrights, trademarks, and service marks of others without their permission can place the user in an untenable and embarrassing position. If there is any doubt whether a particular use of the intellectual property of another will result in liability for infringement, the discreet course of action is to obtain permission.

APPLYING FOR COPYRIGHT

The Copyright Office in Washington, D. C., can provide all forms and information about which forms must be used to protect different kinds of works. Each form is accompanied by line-by-line instructions on how to fill it out correctly. This appendix is designed to give you a synopsis of the various forms and the works to which they apply. You can also write for information to:

Information and Publications Section, LM-455
Copyright Office
Library of Congress
Washington, D.C. 20559

Important telephone numbers at the Copyright Office are:

- **Public Information** (*general information*): 202-479-0700
- **Forms and Circulars Hotline** (*obtaining specific application forms or informational publications*): 202-707-9100
- **Reference and Bibliography:** 202-707-6850
- **Certifications and Documents** (*certified copies of registra-*

tions and other copyright-related documents in office records): 202-707-6787

- **Copyright General Counsel's Office** *(legal questions):* 202-707-8380
- **Document Unit** *(recording of assignments and other copyright-related documents):* 202-707-1759
- **Licensing Division** (questions on various compulsory licenses): 202-707-8150

Which Copyright Form Should You Use?

Form TX

When to Use: Use to register published or unpublished non-dramatic literary works, excluding periodicals or serial issues. This class includes a wide variety of works: fiction, non-fiction, poetry, textbooks, reference works, directories, catalogs, advertising copy, compilations of information, and computer programs.

Deposit to Accompany Application: Must be accompanied by a deposit consisting of copies or phonorecords representing the entire work for which the registration is to be made. The following are the general deposit requirements:

- *Unpublished Work:* Deposit one complete copy (or phonorecord).
- *Published Work:* Deposit two complete copies (or phonorecords) of the best edition.
- *Work First Published Outside of the U.S.:* Deposit one complete copy (or phonorecord) of the first foreign edition.
- *Contribution to a Collective Work:* Deposit one complete copy (or phonorecord) of the best edition of the collective work.

Form SE

When to Use: Use a separate Form SE for registration of each individual issue of a serial, Class SE. A serial is defined as a work issued or intended to be issued in successive parts bearing numerical or chronological designations and intended to be continued indefinitely. This class includes a variety of works: periodicals; newspapers; annuals; the journals, proceedings, transactions, etc., of societies. Do not use Form SE to register an individual contribution to a serial. Use Form TX for such contributions.

Deposit to Accompany Application: Must be accompanied by a deposit consisting of copies or phonorecords representing the entire work for which registration is to be made. The following are the general deposit requirements:

Deposit two complete copies (or phonorecords) of the best edition.

Work first Published Outside the United States: Deposit one complete copy (or phonorecord) of the first foreign edition.

Form VA

When to Use: Use to register published or unpublished works of the visual arts. This category consists of "pictorial, graphic, or sculptural works," including two-dimensional and three-dimensional works of fine, graphic, and applied art, photographs, prints and art reproductions, maps, globes, charts, technical drawings diagrams, and models.

What Does Copyright Protect: Copyright in a work of visual arts protects those pictorial, graphic, or sculptural elements that, either alone or in combination, represent an "original work of authorship." The law declares: "In no case does copyright protection for an original work of authorship extend to any idea, procedure, process, system, method of operation, concept, principle, or discovery, regardless of the form in which it is described, explained, illustrated, or embodied in such work."

Works of Artistic Craftsmanship and Designs; "Works of artistic craftsmanship" are registrable on Form VA, but the law makes clear that protection extends to "their form" and not to "their mechanical or utilitarian aspects." The "design of a useful article" is considered copyrightable "only if, and only to the extent that, such design incorporates pictorial, graphic, or sculptural features that can be identified separately from, and are capable of existing independently of, the utilitarian aspects of the article."

Labels and Advertisements: Works prepared for use in connection with the sale or advertisement of goods and services are registrable if they contain "original work of authorship." Use Form VA if the copyrightable material in the work you are registering is mainly pictorial or graphic; use Form TX if it consists mainly of text. NOTE: Words and short phrases such as names, titles, and slogans cannot be protected by copyright, and the same is true of standard symbols, emblems, and other commonly used graphic designs that are in the public domain. When used commercially, material of that sort can sometimes be protected under state laws of unfair competition or under Federal trademark laws. For information about trademark registration, write to the Commissioner of Patents and Trademarks, Washington, D.C. 20231.

Deposit to Accompany Application: Must be accompanied by a deposit consisting of copies representing the entire work for which registration is to be made.

- *Unpublished Work:* Deposit one complete copy.
- *Published Work:* Deposit two complete copies of the best edition.
- *Work First Published Outside the United States:* Deposit one complete copy of the first foreign edition.
- *Contribution to a Collective Work:* Deposit one complete copy of the best edition of the collective work.

Form SR

When to Use: Use to register published or unpublished sound recordings. It should be used where the copyright claim is limited to the sound recording itself, and may be used where the same copyright claimant is seeking simultaneous registration of the underlying musical, dramatic, or literary work embodied in the phonorecord.

With one exception, "sound recordings" are works that result from the fixation of a series of musical, spoken, or other sounds. The exception is for the audio portions of audiovisual works, such as a motion picture soundtrack or an audio cassette accompanying a filmstrip; these are considered a part of the audiovisual work as a whole.

Deposit to Accompany Application: Must be accompanied by a deposit consisting of phonorecords representing the entire work for which registration is to be made.

- *Unpublished Work:* Deposit one complete phonorecord.
- *Published Work:* Deposit two complete phonorecords of the best edition, together with "any printed or other visually perceptible material" published with the phonorecords.
- *Work First Published Outside the U.S.:* Deposit one complete phonorecord of the first foreign edition.
- *Contribution to a Collective Work:* Deposit one complete phonorecord of the best edition of the collective work.

Form PA

When to Use: Use to register published or unpublished works of the performing arts. This class includes works prepared for the purpose of being "performed" directly before an audience or indirectly "by means of any device or process." Works of the performing arts include: (1) musical works, including any accompanying words; (2) dramatic works, including any accompanying music; (3) pantomimes and choreographic works; and (4) motion pictures and other audiovisual works.

Deposit to Accompany Application: Must be accompanied by a deposit consisting of copies or phonorecords representing the entire work for which registration is to be made. The following are the general deposit requirements:

- *Unpublished Work:* One complete copy (or phonorecord).

- *Published Work:* Deposit two complete copies (or phono-records) of the best edition.
- *Work First Published Outside the United States:* Deposit one complete copy (or phonorecord) of the first foreign edition.
- *Contribution to a Collective Work:* Deposit one complete copy (or phonorecord) of the best edition of the collective work.
- *Motion Pictures:* Deposit *both* of the following: (1) a separate written description of the contents of the motion picture; and (2) for a published work, one complete copy of the best edition of the motion picture; or, for an unpublished work, one complete copy of the motion picture or identifying material. Identifying material may be either an audiorecording of the entire soundtrack or one frame enlargement or similar visual print from each ten-minute segment.

Some definitions to clarify the above:
"Works": "Works are the basic subject matter of copyright; they are what authors create and copyright protects. The law draws a sharp distinction between the "work" and "any material object in which the work is embodied."
"Copies" and "Phonorecords": These are the two types of material objects in which "works" are embodied. In general, "copies" are objects from which a work can be read or visually perceived, directly or with the aid of a machine or device, such as manuscripts, books, sheet music, film, and videotape. "Phonorecords" are objects embodying fixations of sounds, such as audio tapes and phonograph disks. For example, a song (the "work") can be reproduced in sheet music ("copies") or phonograph disks ("phonorecords"), or both.
"Sound Recordings": These are "works," not "copies" or "phonorecords." "Sound recordings" are "works that result from the fixation of a series of musical, spoken, or other sounds, but not including the sounds accompanying a motion picture or other audiovisual work." Example: When a record

company issues a new release, the release will typically involve two distinct "works": the "musical work" that has been recorded, and the "sound recording" as a separate work in itself. The material objects that the record company sends out are "phonorecords": physical reproductions of both the "musical work" and the "sound recording."

Mailing Requirements:

It is important that you send the application, the deposit copy or copies, and the $10 fee together in the same envelope or package. The Copyright Office cannot process them unless they are received together. Send to: Register of Copyrights, Library of Congress, Washington, D.C. 20559.

APPENDIX B

OBTAINING PERMISSION TO REPRODUCE COPY- RIGHTED WORKS

The first step is to contact the copyright owner named on any copyright notice in the work. If the named copyright owner cannot be located, the Copyright Office will conduct a search of its records as to copyright status for a fee of $10 per hour. A copyright search may be useful in the case of a significant work produced by an industry in which the copyright proprietors are in the habit of obtaining copyright registrations— for a book, a motion picture, a television program, etc. The Copyright Office search approach may be less useful for the types of works which likely were not subject to separate copyright registration, like photographs or magazine articles.

Information on the status of copyright in musical works can frequently be obtained from the performing rights societies:

ASCAP
ASCAP Building
One Lincoln Plaza
New York, New York 10023
(212) 595-3050

BMI
320 West 57th Street
New York, New York 10019
(212) 586-2000

SESAC
156 West 56th Street
New York, New York 10019
(212) 586-3450

These organizations can also provide information about obtaining blanket licenses or licenses limited to a single identified copyrighted musical composition.

APPENDIX C

APPLYING FOR STATE REGISTRATION OF TRADE AND SERVICE MARKS

Here are the addresses and telephone numbers for the state organizations to contact in regard to state trademark and service mark registrations.

Alabama
Secretary of State
State House, Room 208
11 S. Union Street
Montgomery, AL 36130
(205) 261-7200

Alaska
Department of Commerce
   and Economic Development
State Office Building, 9th
   Floor
333 Willoughby Avenue
Mail to: P.O. Box D
Juneau, AK 99811
(907) 465-2500

Arizona
Secretary of State
State Capitol,
   West Wing
1700 W. Washington Street
Phoenix, AZ 85007
(602) 255-4285

Arkansas
Secretary of State
State Capitol,
   Room 256
5th & Woodlane
Little Rock, AR 72201
(501) 371-1010

California
Secretary of State
Public Market Building
1230 J Street
Sacramento, CA 95814
(916) 445-6371

Colorado
Secretary of State
Department of State
One Civic Center Plaza,
   Room 200
1560 Broadway
Denver, CO 80202
(303) 866-2762

Connecticut
Secretary of State
State Capitol, Room 106
210 Capitol Avenue
Hartford, CT 06106
(203) 566-2739

Delaware
Secretary of State
Department of State
Townsend Building
Loockerman & Federal
   Streets
Dover, DE 19901
(302) 736-4111

Florida
Secretary of State
Department of State
The Capitol, Plaza Level II
Tallahassee, FL 32399-0250
(904) 488-3680

Georgia
Secretary of State
State Capitol, Room 214
Atlanta, GA 30334
(404) 656-2881

Hawaii
Department of Commerce
   and Consumer Affairs
Kamamalu, 2nd Floor
1010 Richards Street
Mail to: P.O. Box 541
Honolulu, HI 96809
(808) 548-7505

Idaho
Secretary of State
State Capitol Building
Room 203
700 W. Jefferson Street
Boise, ID 83720
(208) 334-2300

Illinois
Secretary of State
State Capitol, Room 213
Springfield, IL 62706
(217) 782-2201

Indiana
Secretary of State
State House, Room 201
200 W. Washington Street
Indianapolis, IN 46204
(317) 232-6531

Iowa
Secretary of State
Corporations Division
State Capitol Building
10th Street & Grand Avenue

Des Moines, IA 50319
(515) 281-5864

Kansas
Secretary of State
State Capitol, 2nd Floor
Topeka, KS 66612-1594
(913) 296-2236

Kentucky
Secretary of State
State Capitol Building, Room
  150
Frankfort, KY 40601
(502) 564-3490

Louisiana
Secretary of State
State Capitol, 15th Floor
900 Riverside North
Mail to: P.O. Box 94125
Baton Rouge, LA 70804-
  9125
(504) 342-5710

Maine
Secretary of State
Mail to: State House
  Station 29
Augusta, ME 04333
(207) 289-1090

Maryland
Secretary of State
State House
Annapolis, MD 21401
(301) 974-3421

Massachusetts
Secretary of the
  Commonwealth
State House, Room 337

Beacon Street
Boston, MA 02133
(617) 727-9180

Michigan
Department of Commerce
Law Building
525 W. Ottawa Street
Mail to: P.O. Box 30004
Lansing, MI 48909
(517) 373-7230

Minnesota
Secretary of State
State Office Building, Room
  180
435 Park Street
St. Paul, MN 55155
(612) 296-3266

Mississippi
Secretary of State
Heber Ladner Building
401 Mississippi Street
Mail to: P.O. Box 136
Jackson, MS 39205
(601) 359-1350

Missouri
Secretary of State
Harry S. Truman State
  Office Building
Room 830
301 W. High Street
Mail to: P.O. Box 778
Jefferson City, MO 65102
(314) 751-2379

Montana
Secretary of State
Capitol Building, Room 225

Helena, MT 59620
(406) 444-2034

Nebraska
Secretary of State
State Capitol, Room 2300
Lincoln, NE 68509-4608
(402) 471-2554

Nevada
Secretary of State
Mail to: Capitol Complex
Carson City, NV 89710
(702) 885-5203

New Hampshire
Secretary of State
State House, Room 204
107 N. Main Street
Concord, NH 03301
(603) 271-3242

New Jersey
Secretary of State
State House
125 W. State Street
Mail to: CN 300
Trenton, NJ 08625
(609) 984-1900

New Mexico
Secretary of State
State Capitol, Room 400
Santa Fe, NM 87503
(505) 827-3600

New York
Secretary of State
Department of State
162 Washington Avenue
Albany, NY 12231
(518) 474-4750

North Carolina
Secretary of State
State Capitol
Capitol Square
Raleigh, NC 27611
(919) 733-3433

North Dakota
Secretary of State
State Capitol
Bismarck, ND 58505
(701) 224-2900

Ohio
Secretary of State
30 E. Broad Street, 14th
  Floor
Columbus, OH 43266-0418
(614) 466-2655

Oklahoma
Secretary of State
State Capitol, Room 101
Lincoln Boulevard
Oklahoma City, OK 73105
(405) 521-3911

Oregon
Secretary of State
State Capitol, Room 136
Salem, OR 97310
(503) 378-4139

Pennsylvania
Secretary of the
  Commonwealth
Executive Office
Department of State
North Office Building,
  Room 302
Commonwealth Avenue &
  North Street

Harrisburg, PA 17120
(717) 787-7630

Rhode Island
Secretary of State
Department of State
State House, Room 217
82 Smith Street
Providence, RI 02903
(401) 277-2357

South Carolina
Secretary of State
Wade Hampton Office
   Building
Capitol Complex
Mail to: P.O. Box 11350
Columbia, SC 29211
(803) 734-2170

South Dakota
Secretary of State
State Capitol
500 E. Capitol Avenue
Pierre, SD 57501-5077
(605) 773-3537

Tennessee
Secretary of State
State Capitol, 1st Floor
Nashville, TN 37219
(615) 741-2816

Texas
Secretary of State
Executive Department
Capitol Building, Room 127
11th & Congress
Mail to: P.O. Box 12697,
   Capitol Station
Austin, TX 78711
(512) 463-5701

Utah
Director
Licensing (Corporate)
Corporations & Uniform
   Commercial Code Div.
Department of Business
   Regulation
Heber M. Wells Building
160 East 300 South
Salt Lake City, UT 84145-
   0801
(801) 530-6027

Vermont
Secretary of State
Redstone Building
26 Terrace Street
Montpelier, VT 05602
(802) 828-2363

Virginia
Director of Administration
Licensing (Corporate)
State Corporation
   Commission
1220 Bank Street
Mail to: P.O. Box 1197
Richmond, VA 23219
(804) 786-4642

Washington
Secretary of State
Legislative Building
Capitol Campus
Mail to: Mail Stop AS-22
Olympia, WA 98504
(206) 753-7121 & 753-7124

West Virginia
Secretary of State
State Capitol, Room W. 157

Charleston, WV 25305
(304) 345-4000

Wisconsin
Secretary of State
General Executive Facility I,
   Room 271
201 E. Washington Avenue
Mail to: P.O. Box 7848
Madison, WI 53707
(608) 266-5801

Wyoming
Secretary of State
State Capitol, Room 106
200 W. 24th Street
Cheyenne, WY 82002-0020
(307) 777-7378

INTERNATIONAL CLASSIFI-CATION OF GOODS AND SERVICES UNDER THE LANHAM ACT

Goods

1. Chemical products used in industry, science, photography, agriculture, horticulture, forestry; artificial and synthetic resins; plastics in the form of powders, liquids or pastes, for industrial use; manures (natural and artificial); fire extinguishing compositions; tempering substances and chemical preparations for soldering; chemical substances for preserving foodstuffs; tanning substances; adhesive substances used in industry.

2. Paints, varnishes, lacquers; preservatives against rust and against deterioration of wood; coloring matters, dyestuffs; mordants; natural resins; metals in foil and powder form for painters and decorators.

3. Bleaching preparations and other substances for laundry use; cleaning, polishing, scouring and abrasive preparations; soaps; perfumery; essential oils, cosmetics, hair lotions; dentifrices.

4. Industrial oils and greases (other than oils and fats and es-

sential oils); lubricants; dust laying and absorbing compositions; fuels (including motor spirit) and illuminants; candles,
tapers, night lights and wicks.

5. Pharmaceutical, veterinary, and sanitary substances; in-
fants' and invalids' foods; plasters, material for bandaging; material for stopping teeth, dental wax, disinfectants; preparations
for killing weeds and destroying vermin.

6. Unwrought and partly wrought common metals and their
alloys; anchors, anvils, bells, rolled and cast building materials;
rails and other metallic materials for railway tracks; chains (except driving chains for vehicles); cables and wires (nonelectric);
locksmiths' work; metallic pipes and tubes; safes and cash boxes; steel balls; horseshoes; nails and screws; other goods in non-
precious metal not included in other classes; ores.

7. Machines and machine tools; motors (except for land vehicles); machine couplings and belting (except for land vehicles); large size agricultural implements; incubators.

8. Hand tools and instruments; cutlery, forks, and spoons;
side arms.

9. Scientific, nautical, surveying and electrical apparatus and
instruments (including wireless), photographic, cinemato-
graphic, optical, weighing, measuring, signalling, checking (su-
pervision), life-saving and teaching apparatus and instruments;
coin or counterfeed apparatus; talking machines; cash registers;
calculating machines; fire extinguishing apparatus.

10. Surgical, medical, dental, and veterinary instruments and
apparatus (including artificial limbs, eyes, and teeth).

11. Installations for lighting, heating, steam generating,
cooking, refrigerating, drying, ventilating, water supply, and
sanitary purposes.

12. Vehicles; apparatus for locomotion by land, air, or
water.

13. Firearms; ammunition and projectiles; explosive substances; fireworks.

14. Precious metals and their alloys and goods in precious
metals or coated therewith (except cutlery, forks and spoons);
jewelry, precious stones, horological and other chronometric
instruments.

15. Musical instruments (other than talking machines and wireless apparatus).

16. Paper and paper articles, cardboard and cardboard articles; printed matter, newspapers and periodicals, books; bookbinding material; photographs; stationery, adhesive materials (stationery); artists' materials; paint brushes; typewriters and office requisites (other than furniture); instructional and teaching material (other than apparatus); playing cards; printers' type and cliches (stereotype).

17. Gutta percha, india rubber, balata and substitutes, articles made from these substances and not included in other classes; plastics in the form of sheets, blocks and rods, being for use in manufacture; materials for packing, stopping or insulating; asbestos, mica and their products; hose pipes (nonmetallic).

18. Leather and imitations of leather, and articles made from these materials and not included in other classes; skins, hides; trunks and travelling bags; umbrellas, parasols and walking sticks; whips, harness and saddlery.

19. Building materials, natural and artificial stone, cement, lime, mortar, plaster and gravel; pipes of earthenware or cement; roadmaking materials; asphalt, pitch and bitumen; portable buildings; stone monuments; chimney pots.

20. Furniture, mirrors, picture frames; articles (not included in other classes) of wood, cork, reeds, cane, wicker, horn, bone, ivory, whalebone, shell, amber, mother-of-pearl, meerschaum, celluloid, substitutes for all these materials, or of plastics.

21. Small domestic utensils and containers (not of precious metals, or coated therewith); combs and sponges; brushes (other than paint brushes), brushmaking materials; instruments and material for cleaning purposes, steel wool; unworked or semi-worked glass (excluding glass used in building); glassware, porcelain and earthenware, not included in other classes.

22. Ropes, string, nets, tents, awnings, tarpaulins, sails, sacks; padding and stuffing materials (hair, kapok, feathers, seaweed, etc.); raw fibrous textile materials.

23. Yarns, threads.

24. Tissues (piece goods); bed and table covers; textile articles not included in other classes.

25. Clothing, including boots, shoes and slippers.

26. Lace and embroidery, ribands and braid; buttons, press buttons, hooks and eyes, pins and needles; artificial flowers.

27. Carpets, rugs, mats and matting; linoleums and other materials for covering existing floors; wall hangings (nontextile).

28. Games and playthings; gymnastic and sporting articles (except clothing); ornaments and decorations for Christmas trees.

29. Meats, fish, poultry and game; meat extracts; preserved, dried and cooked fruits and vegetables; jellies, jams; eggs, milk and other dairy products; edible oils and fats; preserves, pickles.

30. Coffee, tea, cocoa, sugar, rice, tapioca, sago, coffee substitutes; flour, and preparations made from cereals; bread, biscuits, cakes, pastry and confectionery, ices; honey, treacle; yeast, baking powder; salt, mustard, pepper, vinegar, sauces, spices; ice.

31. Agricultural, horticultural and forestry products and grains not included in other classes; living animals, fresh fruits and vegetables; seeds; live plants and flowers; foodstuffs for animals, malt.

32. Beer, ale and porter; mineral and aerated waters and other nonalcoholic drinks; syrups and other preparations for making beverages.

33. Wines, spirits and liqueurs.

34. Tobacco, raw or manufactured; smokers' articles; matches.

Services

35. Advertising and business.

36. Insurance and financial.

37. Construction and repair.

38. Communication.
39. Transportation and storage.
40. Material treatment.
41. Education and entertainment.
42. Miscellaneous.

INDEX